The New Trail of Tears

NAOMI SCHAEFER RILEY

The New
Trail of Tears

How Washington Is Destroying

American Indians

 ENCOUNTER BOOKS

NEW YORK · LONDON

First American edition published in 2016 by Encounter Books, an activity of Encounter for Culture and Education, Inc., a nonprofit, tax exempt corporation.
Encounter Books website address: www.encounterbooks.com

Manufactured in the United States and printed on acid-free paper. The paper used in this publication meets the minimum requirements of ANSI/NISO Z39.48–1992 (R 1997) (*Permanence of Paper*).

FIRST AMERICAN EDITION

LIBRARY OF CONGRESS CATALOGING-IN-PUBLICATION DATA

Names: Riley, Naomi Schaefer, author.
Title: The new Trail of Tears: how Washington is destroying American Indians /Naomi Schaefer Riley.
Other titles: How Washington is destroying American Indians
Description: New York: Encounter Books, [2016] | Includes bibliographical references and index.
Identifiers: LCCN 2015037589 | ISBN 9781594038532 (hardcover: alk. paper) | ISBN 9781594038549 (ebook)
Subjects: LCSH: Indians of North America—Government relations. | Indians of North America—Social conditions. | Indians of North America—Politics and government.
Classification: LCC E93 .R55 2016 | DDC 323.1197--DC23
LC record available at http://lccn.loc.gov/2015037589

CONTENTS

What Does America Owe Indians?

WHEN MY DAUGHTER was in second grade, she came home with what seemed like a typical assignment. Asked to read about how the Dutch swindled Native Americans into giving up Manhattan for a pile of beads, she then had to write a paragraph about how the Natives must have felt. This exercise in empathy was puzzling for her and I presume millions of other schoolchildren receiving similar instructions – not to mention their parents. There's rarely much context to these lessons. But more importantly, there's little sense in our school curricula that American Indians are anything more than a historic artifact.

Most Americans know nothing about what life is like for the 3 million Indians today, particularly the 1 million living on reservations. If you ask people what ails American Indians, they'll be quick to tell you about what white people did to them 100, 200, or 400 years ago. Americans who read a newspaper might come across articles every once in a while about suicide or poverty on reservations. They might see stories about rape or child abuse or alcoholism. And sometimes they might take note of a casino being built on Indian land. But these stories are typically so depressing that most of us would rather turn our heads and turn the page.

According to statistics compiled from various federal agencies, American Indians have the highest rate of *poverty* of any racial group in the nation – almost twice the national average.[1] This deprivation seems to contribute not only to higher rates of crime but also to higher rates of suicide, alcoholism, gang membership, and sexual abuse. In 2011, the suicide rate for Native American men ages 15–24 was 57% higher than for the general population.[2] (*Suicide* is also the leading cause of death for Native American males aged 10 to 14.) Alcohol-use disorders are more likely among American Indian youths than those belonging to other racial groups.[3] Involvement in gang activity is more prevalent among Native Americans than it is among Latinos and African Americans.[4] Native American women report being raped two and half times as often as the national average.[5] The rate of child abuse among Native Americans is twice as high as the national average.[6] What's more, each of these problems is statistically worse when the results are restricted to Native Americans who live on reservations. For example, an estimated one out of every four girls and one out of every six boys in Indian country is molested before the age of 18.[7]

It's no wonder most Americans would rather not think about this population. The United States is the wealthiest nation on earth, but we have what amounts to a third world country within our borders. Critics like to say it's easy for the wealthy to ignore the problems of our inner cities because the wealthy can simply avoid these neighborhoods. It's even easier for the wealthy to ignore the problems of Indian reservations in South Dakota and Montana, because they never have to think about these neighborhoods, much less see them from the window of a train or a car.

By the time most American students get to college and take courses in ethnic studies, they learn that what ails American Indians is their history. Indians' decades – centuries – of victimization at the hands of whites are only being compounded by non-Indians' perpetual insensitivity. And if only we could somehow return Indians to their state of nature, "pre-Contact," professors tell students, Indians would be saved. Barring that, though, there's little we can do.

This kind of education tends to lead people to two conclusions. The first is that America should give Indians as much money as possible from the federal coffers. It's only fair that the nation make good on its promises to provide for them. And really, it should do more than that. It should offer some kind of reparations for the harm inflicted upon Indians by westward expansion, by wars, by racism, and by the reservation system.

The second is that we should make sure that American Indians don't have to continue to suffer the indignities of having their culture mocked or degraded. So we should seek out any form of the old way of thinking about Indians and eradicate it.

To deal with the question of money first: The two primary agencies charged with overseeing the activities of the roughly 1 million Indians who live on reservations – the Bureau of Indian Affairs (BIA) and the Bureau of Indian Education (BIE), both part of the Department of the Interior – have a total of 9,000 employees. That's one employee for every 111 Indians on a reservation. According to a report from the Cato Institute, federal funding for these agencies' various subsidy programs – which cover programs for education, economic development, tribal courts, road maintenance, agriculture, and social services – was almost $3 billion in 2015. About $850 million of this is the BIE's share for providing for its 42,000 students (most children on reservations don't attend BIE schools), which amounts to about $20,000 per pupil,[8] compared to a national average of $12,400.[9]

But that's not all. As the report from the Cato Institute notes, "Aside from the BIA and BIE, many other federal agencies have subsidy programs for American Indians. The Department of Health and Human Services houses the Indian Health Service, which has a budget of about $4 billion. The Department of Housing and Urban Development runs the Native American Housing Block Grant Program, which has a budget of about $800 million. And the Department of Education spends more than $300 million a year on BIE schools."[10]

What have American Indians gotten for all this money? Not much, it seems. It's not just that the education these children receive is deplorable. The BIE can't even keep the buildings from falling down. As John Kline, a Republican congressman from Minnesota, explained at a hearing in May 2015, "You've got collapsing roofs, leaking roofs, buckling floors, exposed wires, popping circuit breakers, gas leaks. That's totally unacceptable." He noted, "You can't be well-educated, in my opinion, when you're attending school wearing your coat, wearing your mittens and hoping that the blanket keeps out the 30-degree below-zero air."[11]

Kline is right, but most observers seem to agree it's largely a problem of management, not money, that has gotten the BIE to where it is today. The agency is on its 36th director in 33 years. To address the crumbling infrastructure, in the budget for 2016 the Obama administration asked for $1 billion for the BIE. But if the past is any guide, it's unlikely that things will change.

As for sensitivity to the cultural and historical plight of Indians, what we teach our children in schools typically is the history of white encounters with Indians over a hundred years ago. A study by Sarah Shear, a professor at the University of Missouri, found that 87 percent of references to American Indians in state academic standards portrayed them in a pre-1900 context. According to Shear, when students arrive in her college classroom, they're largely ignorant about modern Indians. "What they told me is that they learned about Thanksgiving and Columbus Day," she told a writer for the Indian Country website. "Every once in a while, a student would mention something about the Trail of Tears. It was incredibly frustrating. They were coming to college believing that all Indians are dead."[12]

Even when states adopt formal standards to address the issue of Native American history, the content is typically about the raping and pillaging of Indian communities in the past. Take Utah's curriculum on Indians, which teaches high-school students about the five major tribes found there today. Of the Navajos, for instance, students will learn:

> *In the winter of 1863/1864, after their crops, livestock, and homes had been destroyed by the United States Army under Christopher "Kit" Carson, over 8,000 Navajos were forced to walk twelve-to-fifteen miles a day – with little food and little or no protection from the winter weather – from their ancestral homelands to the remote and desolate Bosque Redondo Reservation. The memory of the Long Walk has haunted generations of Navajos, and the story of the Long Walk is important to the history of Utah's Navajos. Some Navajos were able to escape the army and moved into what is now southeastern Utah.*[13]

To the extent they're even paying attention, most American children's knowledge of the history of American Indians will include starvation, death by diseases brought from Europe, and massacres at the hands of white settlers. All of which is certainly true. (They'll rarely hear about the brutalities that Indians committed against white settlers, however.) These students will come to see Indians as people who lived off the land and worshipped nature – our first environmentalists, perhaps. Indeed, there are those who'll take from their lessons that the people indigenous to North America are to be emulated in modern times because of their respect for the earth and its creatures.

Schoolchildren commonly learn the words of Chief Seattle, who allegedly wrote to the U.S. government in 1851: "The President in Washington sends word that he wishes to buy our land. But how can you buy or sell the sky? the land? The idea is strange to us. If we do not own the freshness of the air and the sparkle of the water, how can you buy them? Every part of this earth is sacred to my people. Every shining pine needle, every sandy shore, every mist in the dark woods, every clearing and humming insect is holy in the memory and experience of my people."

As Fergus Bordewich notes in his book *Killing the White Man's Indian*, "More than any other single document, Seattle's words lend support to the increasingly common belief that, to Indians, any disruption or commercialization of the earth's natural order is sacrilege and that the most moral, the most truly 'Indian,' relationship with the land is a kind of poetic passivity. Seattle has achieved a kind of prophetic stature among environmentalists." Too bad much of this mythology is complete bunk. The earliest version of the speech was composed in 1887 "from memory" by a white doctor who claimed to have been present at its delivery. The most commonly reproduced version was actually written in 1972 "by Ted Perry, a Texas scriptwriter, to serve as narration for a film produced by Southern Baptist Radio and Television Commission, which wished to give its audience a warning about the environment."[14]

The use of such stories probably does more to assuage white guilt than it does to alleviate the problems plaguing Indians. The real question is this: if not sensitivity and money, what does America owe Indians?

In the past two years, I've traveled to Indian communities around the United States and Canada. I've interviewed tribal leaders, economists, educators, businesspeople, and government officials, all in an effort to understand what ails American Indians, particularly those on reservations. The results are by no means a comprehensive history of American Indians or even a complete picture of American Indians today. There are 562 federally recognized Indian nations in the United States – about half of which are in Alaska – and 310 reservations. Any book about American Indians will have to make some generalizations. And for that I apologize in advance. But the fact that these groups have different cultural traditions, different treaties, and different economic, political, and social situations doesn't mean they have nothing in common.

As you'll see in this book, the problems American Indians face today – lack of economic opportunity, lack of education, and lack of equal protection under the law – and the solutions to these problems require a different approach from the misguided paternalism of the past 150 years. It's not the history of forced assimilation, war, and mass murder that have left American Indians in a deplorable state; it's the federal government's policies today. These policies were begun by officials who didn't know or didn't care about what might help Indians; today they're carried on by officials who claim to care but can't seem to grasp the problems these policies are causing.

The tragedy of America's Indian policies demands immediate examination – not only because they make the lives of millions of American citizens harder and more dangerous but also because they're a microcosm of everything that has gone wrong with modern liberalism. They're the result of decades of politicians and bureaucrats showering a victimized people with money and sensitivity instead of what they truly need – the autonomy, the education, and the legal protections to improve their own situations. American Indians, like all Americans, must be able to avail themselves of the economic and legal freedoms this country guarantees. Until then, they'll remain mired in poverty, social pathology, and the kind of anger that comes from knowing that your fate is controlled by ill-informed and ineffective bureaucracies.

What America really owes Indians is nothing less than the opportunity to live lives of freedom and dignity in the land we all share.

PART ONE

The False Promise of Sovereignty

CHAPTER ONE

Someone Else's Responsibility

Property Rights as Native Rights

"IT'S FREE MONEY!" a Crow legislator by the name of Karl Little Owl tells Ivan Small. Small, an older man who has known Little Owl since he was a child, laughs skeptically. "Really? How's that?"

"We didn't have to spend a dime of the tribe's funds on this."

"A good thing," Small replies, chuckling, "since the tribe doesn't have any money."

We're standing just outside a tent where a ceremony to mark the breaking of ground on Apsaalooke Warrior Apartments is about to begin. The first development project on the Crow reservation in about a decade, Apsaalooke Warrior Apartments will be a 15-bed veterans' home perched on a hill overlooking Crow Agency, the reservation's political center. A couple of miles from the battlefield where Custer made his last stand, the home will no doubt be a reminder of Indians' Pyrrhic victory here in Montana and the fact that it was short-lived. Soon after the Battle of the Little Bighorn, the U.S. Army succeeded in removing the remaining Indians from their land and putting them on reservations. In recent times, the policies that resulted in the mass

3

extinguishment of Indian lives have been replaced by policies that result in their mass impoverishment and an existence circumscribed by violence and tragedy.

Here, under the tent, though, there's great celebration. Representatives of the Bureau of Indian Affairs, the state of Montana, and the tribal leadership are present. One person after another takes the podium to congratulate the individuals who spearheaded this development, applied for the grants, and waded through the bureaucratic morass (though no one dares call it that) to get this project off the ground. After about a dozen speeches, the four tribal leaders don feathered bonnets and sing a traditional song in their native language. Then each takes a golden shovel and turns over a piece of the soil.

At a cost of just under $8 million, the development wouldn't have been possible without a combination of federal, state, and private donations. The Crow tribe is broke, as Small observes, for a variety of reasons. There's next to no economic activity on the reservation. In this desolate area in southeastern Montana, the unemployment rate is 47 percent (when you include people who have given up looking for jobs).[1] The people who *are* employed almost all work for the tribal government.

And then there's this: the tribe, according to its leadership, owes the Department of Housing and Urban Development about $3 million. In the 1990s, HUD built most of the homes on the reservation, and the tribal leadership promised to exact a small monthly payment from each homeowner. Conrad Stewart, who used to work in the tribal housing office and now chairs the Natural Resources Infrastructure Committee for the Crow tribe, says that the payments were to be between $20 and $30 a month.

But then the tribe members, among them people in Small's own extended family, refused to pay. Instead, Stewart says, "When the tribe tried to go and recoup some of the money, they made threats. They said the tribe should pay for this. And the tribe has been paying for it [ever since]."

Now the situation is getting bleaker. HUD, the tribal leaders tell me, refuses to build any more homes until the money is paid back.

And so no homes are being constructed or repaired. Instead more and more people are moving into each small trailer home. The result is that 75 percent of tribal members between the ages of 18 and 40 "don't have homes," according to Stewart.

Stewart blames part of this problem on the tribal government's lack of forethought. "They were thinking about the short term, because a lot of times the administration – they campaigned and then they got that one year to do something. Well, the next year it's campaign season again." Tribal governance was no doubt an issue here. And the Crow tribe has taken steps to improve the situation. In 2001, it instituted four-year terms instead of two-year terms for the chair and other executive positions. "Now we have three years of business and one year of campaigning," notes Stewart with forced optimism.

Even so, when the tribal government attempted to pass legislation that would require people to pay their debt to HUD, Stewart says, the "old-timers" were telling people, "You do this and then they're going to take all our homes and then they're going to kick everybody out on the streets. Everyone will be homeless." Fourteen versions of the financial protection and procedures laws intended to address this situation were reviewed before one was passed. Says Stewart of this legislative ordeal: "These people would cut your throat."

Of course, for anyone with a basic understanding of economics and political science, nothing in this story is surprising. If your political representative is also your landlord and you don't feel like paying your rent, you'll vote him out of office. But when you do that, it'll affect both your own ability to get credit and others' ability to convince someone to build them a home.

But what choice do Crows have? Almost no one on the reservation can afford to build a home, because no one can get a mortgage. And no one can get a mortgage because the property on the reservation is held "in trust" by the federal government and most of it's "owned" communally by the tribe. Which means, effectively, that no bank could ever foreclose on a property, because the bank can't own reservation land.

Even town centers on many Indian reservations are desolate places. Small says there are fewer shops now in Lame Deer, Montana, the capital of the Northern Cheyenne reservation, than there were when he was growing up. There's a small casino – the size of a suburban house – just outside of town. Few non-Indians have a reason to come through Lame Deer, however, so the dozen or so customers at the casino are almost all Indians. These gamblers are effectively taking money given to them by the tribal government for food or housing and giving it back to the tribe through its slot machines.

And the leaders in Lame Deer don't seem particularly interested in bringing more visitors to town. Winfield Russell, vice president of the Northern Cheyenne tribal council, complains to me about the 18-wheelers that use the town's main road to avoid the interstates. But rather than a rest stop (which would bring the tribe some revenue), he shows me a design for a new traffic pattern that will discourage truckers from using the road at all.

Small and I spend three days driving around southeastern Montana together. The early May scenery is beautiful and yet somehow depressing as the occasional snow flurry falls. But every few miles, we come upon a group of 10 to 30 trailer homes that, as anyone can see, are a blight on the land. Broken-down cars and trucks are scattered outside the homes like crushed soda cans. Many homes' windows are broken, with only a kind of tarp separating the residents from the elements. (Residents say they're waiting for HUD to come fix things.) Children's toys are piled up haphazardly, mixed with lawn chairs and trash. Menacing stray dogs roam everywhere, searching for food.

"A man's home is his castle," Small mutters over and over as we survey these neighborhoods. Sometimes he laughs. A big man, with darkened skin and a full head of white hair, Small sometimes seems angry. But mostly he looks tired.

As we drive through the Crow and Cheyenne reservations, Small points out the places he and his extended family have lived. He has spent most of his life here. His mother was Crow and his father was

Northern Cheyenne. He grew up with his six siblings on a farm. Their house had no running water. He's somewhat nostalgic, though: "At least, back then, there wasn't so much crime." Violent crime on the country's 310 reservations is on average about 2.5 times as high as the national average.[2] Fueling the crime are alcohol and drugs – methamphetamines, especially. But Small thinks there's too little law enforcement, both from the federal government and from the tribe itself.

Each morning I set out with Small, he stops in Lame Deer. The town contains a gas station, a half-stocked supermarket, a Catholic church, a school, and a coffee shop. On the first morning we arrive, the woman making Small his latte tells us that the shop was robbed the night before. The culprit stole all the candy in the glass display case, as well as five left flip-flops from a shelf full of gift items. "At least it won't be hard to find him," another customer jokes, imitating a man hobbling on one foot.

The same dark sense of humor pervades the conversation about the condition of the reservations, particularly among older residents. They've seen it all before, and they don't expect anything to get better. Small, who owns some land and a few head of cattle, recently tried to buy land from a neighbor of his on the Crow reservation. The two had agreed on the price. But the Bureau of Indian Affairs blocked the deal. The BIA had recently had land on the reservation appraised as part of a buyback program – the federal government was going to trade one plot of land to the tribe for another – and the appraiser had put a higher value on the land than the price that Small and his neighbor had agreed upon. In fact, as Small tells it, the BIA told the appraiser to overvalue the land so as not to "screw the Indians."

Small is past the point of anger, though, and he laughs. He's no economist, but he's well aware, as he tells me, "Land is worth what someone will pay for it," not what some outside appraiser decides.

Similar stories could be told about jobs, health care, and land management on reservations. We'd like to think that stricter regulation or larger grants or other forms of government intervention or support would solve the many problems on reservations. But there are too

7

many policies standing in the way of real improvements. It's not only that the Bureau of Indian Affairs and the Bureau of Indian Education are perhaps the most inefficient of all federal bureaucracies. It's not only that Washington officials are far removed from the people they serve – though 90 percent of the staff of these bureaucracies are Indians themselves.[3] It's that the BIA's purpose is unclear.

How did we arrive at this sad state of affairs? Between 1777 and 1871, the federal government signed over 400 treaties with American Indians. In the 1850s, the reservation system was devised as a way of ending the Indian wars and moving Indians off of land that white settlers wanted for farming, ranching, or mining. Tribes agreed to give up the land they occupied and move to reservations in exchange for payments and other benefits. Often, of course, these promises weren't kept.

Tribes often ended up far from their homelands. Not only were their new lands less desirable because they had fewer natural resources, American Indians had no idea how to live on them. But, in small ways, they began to adapt. This evolution in fact was already underway. In his book *Sovereign Nations or Reservations?* Terry Anderson notes, "Even before interaction with Europeans, Indian institutions were evolving as a result of changing resource values and technology. Perhaps as much as any other factor, the horse changed the lives of Indians. With the horse, transportation costs declined significantly as did the costs of harvesting buffalo. The result was that many otherwise sedentary tribes took to a more nomadic life."[4] In principle, there's no reason that tribes couldn't have adapted themselves again to a more sedentary life on the reservation, however unjust the reason they'd wound up there in the first place.

But tribal autonomy had been compromised. American Indian communities' ability to subsist often depended on the federal administrators assigned to each tribe, who treated them like children assigned to their care. For example, Indians weren't permitted to leave reservations in search of food; thus, many tribes needed outside shipments of food and other resources in order to survive. This meant that any small delay of appropriations from the federal government could lead to mass starvation or armed conflict.

Agents were supposed to supervise the relationship between Indians and white settlers – including any commercial activity – but by the late 19th century, their roles had shifted to include the forced assimilation of Indians into American culture. Agents oversaw the education (in English) of Indians, enforced a prohibition on alcohol, and ensured that "no Indian should be idle for want of an opportunity to labor or of instructions as to how to go to work, and, if farm work is not extensive enough to employ all idle hands, some other occupation should be introduced."[5]

Of course, this relationship was understood mostly in racial terms. The late 19th and early 20th centuries saw a popular as well as an academic fascination with racial classification. New waves of immigration from Europe, the post–Civil War period of reconstruction, and the Indian wars out west made white Americans hugely interested in and receptive to all sorts of theories of racial differences. The application of Mendel's genetic theories about dominant and recessive traits in plants to human beings launched a wrongheaded and dangerous foray into eugenics.

From the early 19th century, self-styled scientists had developed all sorts of theories about the inferiority of the Indian race. Samuel George Morton, a Philadelphia patrician who had two medical degrees, hypothesized that skull size was correlated with mental capacity. As a result of his phrenological studies, he concluded: "It must be borne in mind that the Indian is incapable of servitude, and that his spirit sunk at once in captivity, and with it his physical energy [whereas] the more pliant Negro, yielding to his fate and accommodating himself to his condition, bore his heavy burden with comparative ease."[6] One of Morton's successors, Josiah Nott, wrote, "It is vain to talk of civilizing [Indians]. You might as well attempt to change the nature of the buffalo."[7]

Those who didn't see race as destiny, though, had plenty of theories of their own. Many Christian missionaries saw it as their duty to "civilize" American Indians, almost as soon as settlers made contact with Indians – in the 18th century, the founder of Dartmouth College told his sponsors he'd "cure the Natives of their Savage Temper" and "purge all the Indian out" of his Indian students.[8] As Fergus Bordewich says in his book *Killing the White Man's Indian*, "Education was seen by well-intentioned Americans both as a moral imperative and as a practical gateway to modern civilization. However their optimism was often rooted in the naïve conviction that Indians were but blank slates waiting to be inscribed with the vigorous script of American civilization."[9]

Senator Henry Dawes of Massachusetts (who served from 1875 to 1893) wasn't quite so insensitive, though, as Bordewich tells the story. In fact, Dawes considered the history of U.S.-Indian relations to be one "of spoliation, of wars, and of humiliation."[10] More importantly, he believed that Indians had the same capacity for education, independence, and economic success as their white brothers – if only the right policies were put in place.

Dawes proposed to take all the reservation land that was held in common, divide it up among Indians individually, and put the rest up for sale to white settlers. He told a group assembled at Lake Mohonk in upstate New York, "If you will prepare the Indian to take care of himself upon this land that is allotted, you will find the solution to the whole question.... He shall have a home and be a citizen of the United States; shall be one of us, contributing his share to all that goes to make up the strength and glory of citizenship in the United States."[11] After he proposed this allotment, one of his colleagues told the assembly, "I have more than once spoken of Senator Dawes's severalty bill as the act of emancipation for the Indian. I believe when it is passed it will enroll his name with that of Lincoln as an Emancipator of those in bonds."[12]

In 1887, Congress passed the General Allotment Act, known as the Dawes Act, which surveyed Indian lands and divided them into parcels, allowing individual Indians to apply for ownership of plots of land (though many of these parcels weren't actually given over completely). The head of a family could receive 160 acres. People under the age of 18 would receive 40 acres. Indians had four years to select the plot they wanted. After that, the secretary of the interior would select it for them. The federal government would hold the land "in trust" for the Indians, but after 25 years had elapsed, the Indians would own the land outright. Well, almost. According to the language of the Dawes Act, "At the expiration of said period the United States will convey the same by patent to said Indian, or his heirs as aforesaid, in fee, discharged of said trust and free of all charge or incumbrance whatsoever: *Provided*, That the President of the United States may in any case in his discretion extend the period."[13]

There are interesting similarities to the "40 acres and a mule" policy implemented after the Civil War to give freed slaves rights to abandoned land previously owned by slaveholders. Of course, in that case, the land was rarely allotted, and there was no federal money to purchase it for former slaves either. But the connection between owning land and having full citizenship was a strong one. Dawes and his colleagues in Washington clearly believed that if Indians got the former, they'd be entitled to and embrace the responsibilities of the latter. Their confidence in Indians' ability to take their fate into their own hands was striking – and it's a sentiment rarely heard among politicians today.

The wording of the Dawes Act continued:

That upon the completion of said allotments and the patenting of the lands to said allottees, each and every number of the respective bands or tribes of Indians to whom allotments have been made shall have the benefit of and be subject to the laws, both civil and criminal, of the State or Territory in which they may reside; and no Territory shall pass or enforce any law denying any such Indian within its jurisdiction the equal protection of the law. And every Indian born within the territorial limits of the United States to whom allotments shall have been made under the provisions of this act, or under any law or treaty, and every Indian born within the territorial limits of the United States who has voluntarily taken up, within said limits, his residence separate and apart from any tribe of Indians therein, and has adopted the habits of civilized life, is hereby declared to be a citizen of the United States, and is entitled to all the rights, privileges, and immunities of such citizens, whether said Indian has been or not, by birth or otherwise, a member of any tribe of Indians within the territorial limits of the United States without in any manner affecting the right of any such Indian to tribal or other property.[14]

The way the Dawes Act was carried out, though, was not as Dawes or his contemporaries had promised, nor were its effects what they had expected. In some cases, Indians who didn't choose a parcel of land were jailed. Whites often got the best land and sometimes the only land that was adjacent to water sources. Some of the land had been surveyed badly, and so its ownership was unclear. By the time the policy ended in 1934, land under Indian ownership had shrunk by 65 percent.[15]

In 1934, the Indian Reorganization Act placed all the land not held fully by individuals into a "trust." Sometimes known as the Indian New Deal, the Indian Reorganization Act was intended to stem the flow of land out of Indian hands. Land that hadn't already been transferred into fee-simple ownership – that is, land that wasn't owned outright – was put into trust by the federal government. From that point on, the land couldn't be sold to non-Indians, but even land transfers among Indians or between Indians and the tribal government were heavily monitored by the federal government. In fact, as Anderson points out, bureaucratic interests as much as anything have historically driven the U.S. government's Indian policy.[16]

The effects of the trust have been disastrous for economic development on Indian lands. First, because most trust land is held communally, individuals don't want to invest in it, and they can't use it as collateral either. As John Koppisch, a writer at *Forbes*, explains: "This leads to what economists call the tragedy of the commons: If everyone owns the land, no one does. So the result is substandard housing and the barren, rundown look that comes from a lack of investment, over-use, and environmental degradation. It's a look that's common world-wide, wherever secure property rights are lacking – much of Africa and South America, inner city housing projects and rent-controlled apartment buildings in the U.S., Indian reservations."[17]

As one tribal leader describing a similar situation in Canada explained to Koppisch, "Markets haven't been allowed to operate in reserve lands. We've been legislated out of the economy. When you don't have individual property rights, you can't build, you can't be bonded, you can't pass on wealth. A lot of small businesses never get started because people can't leverage property [to raise funds]."[18]

Even if an individual technically holds the land, the fact that it's trust land means that the federal government has a say in how it's used. Which makes it significantly less valuable. A 1992 study by Terry Anderson and Dean Lueck found that agricultural productivity on individual trust lands was 30 to 40 percent less, and on tribal trust lands 80 to 90 percent less, than on fee-simple lands on a reservation, where a given title rests entirely with an individual.[19]

Although tribes have been granted somewhat more power over decisions regarding their land in recent years, "at least four federal agencies are involved in the execution of any energy lease on tribal lands.... Not only does the BIA's trust authority raise the cost of energy development on Indian trust lands, it has a long history of not living up to its fiduciary responsibility of managing Indian trust funds." In 1996, a class-action suit against the BIA for this mismanagement resulted in a settlement of $3.4 billion.[20]

Underlying federal policy are the assumptions that Indians are simply incapable of managing their own affairs and that natural resource development somehow runs contrary to their traditions. Researchers have examined this latter assumption in recent years. In his book *1491: New Revelations of the Americas before Columbus*, Charles Mann looks at the scholarly consensus and concludes that the land was hardly "pristine" before Europeans' arrival. For example, he says of the Amazon rainforests, "The new picture doesn't automatically legitimate burning down the forest. Instead it suggests that for a long time clever people who knew tricks that we have yet to learn used big chunks of Amazonia nondestructively. Faced with an ecological problem, the Indians fixed it. Rather than adapt to Nature, they fixed it."[21]

Another common assumption about Indians today is that they're traditionally communists, sharing all property. But the truth is much more complicated, and historians have found significant evidence of individual and family-held property rights among Indian tribes.

In the 1974 "Boldt" decision, which granted fishing rights to Indians in the Pacific Northwest, presiding judge George Boldt cited the history of Indian fishing in the area in his decision: "Generally, individual Indians had primary use rights in the territory where they resided and permissive use rights in the natal territory (if this was different) or in territories where they had consanguineal kin. Subject to such individual claims, most groups claimed autumn fishing use rights in the waters near to their winter villages. Spring and summer fishing areas were often more distantly located and often were shared with other groups from other villages."[22] Indians invested significant effort in ensuring an adequate supply of fish each year. The idea that prior to whites' arrival, Indians were simply roving bands living off whatever wildlife they happened to come upon and then sharing it equally among themselves runs contrary to history – not to mention everything we know about human ingenuity and human nature.

But it's an idea that continues to dictate public policy.

For today's journalists and historians looking back at the Dawes Act, the problem is clear. As Bordewich wrote, "Like many of his contemporaries in the golden age of capitalism, Dawes perceived private property as an almost magical force, a severe but benevolent taskmaster with transformative power."[23]

The truth of the matter is that Dawes was right – *private property is an almost magical force.* As any survey of world history demonstrates, countries that have adopted private property rights and the rule of law to enforce them are better off by almost every measure. Over the past 200 years, with the spread of capitalism, global per capita income has increased more than tenfold and average life expectancy has more than doubled.

As Leonard Carlson notes in his 1981 book *Indians, Bureaucrats, and Land,* "no student of property rights or, indeed, economic theory will be surprised that the complicated and heavily supervised property right that emerged from allotment led to inefficiencies, corruption and losses for both Indians and society."[24]

In addition to the corruption that dominated the initial process of assigning allotments, there was also the 25-year waiting period before Indians actually owned their plot of land outright. This provision, ostensibly intended to protect Indians from selling their land to rapacious whites before Indians were judged "competent" to know their own interests, had the effect of diminishing the land's value. Imagine that you were broke and someone gave you an acre of land but told you that you had to wait 25 years to sell it. Unless you wanted to start planting vegetables tomorrow, what good would it do you? You couldn't even use it as collateral to get a loan, because technically it wouldn't be yours yet. These kinds of provisions have the effect of sucking the magical powers out of a system of private property.

In other words, Indians have long suffered from what Nobel Prize–winning economist Hernando de Soto has called "dead capital." They may possess a certain amount of land on paper, but they can't put it to use by selling it, buying more to take advantage of economies of scale, or borrowing against it.

"There are, of course, arguments that the allotment experiment was a failure because it transferred so much land to whites," notes Anderson, "but there is no systematic evidence to test this proposition. Certainly vast amounts of land were transferred to whites, but by itself this is not prima facie evidence that Indians were left worse off. If land was taken without compensation, there is no doubt that Indians were disadvantaged. To determine the impact of voluntary sales, we would have to know the sale price relative to the value of the land to Indians had it been retained by them."[25]

In other words, if you had a piece of land and you sold it for fair market value, no one would look at the situation and suggest that you had suffered some kind of great loss or had been swindled. You might simply have decided that the money you could get was more valuable to you than the land. Particularly when it comes to farmland, this determination is often based on how large a plot of land you own. Agricultural productivity is based on economies of scale. A reasonable person, whether Indian or non-Indian, might decide that 160 acres isn't enough to make farming worth it or might rather have the money from the sale of the land and do something else with it. Not everyone aspires to be a farmer. But the Dawes Act, as it was written, didn't take sufficient account of these possibilities, and those who assess its success or failure today typically don't either.

If the idea behind U.S. policy in the early 20th century was either to help Indians or to help white settlers, the easiest way of accomplishing this would've been to grant a simple title to the land to either group and let each do what they wanted. But, "had the land been given directly to Indians or whites, what role would there have been for the Office of Indian Affairs?" Anderson asks pointedly. Although the Dawes Act was ostensibly implemented with the idea of making Indians independent and regular citizens of the United States, Washington's oversight of them increased significantly the longer the policy was in place. From 1900 to 1920, the number of employees grew from 101 to 262.[26] (Today, there are about 9,000 employees at the Bureau of Indian Affairs and the Bureau of Indian Education.) This result, says Anderson, "is hardly surprising as bureaucrats are highly unlikely to sit back and watch their mission and jobs wither.... The BIA found its raison d'être with the passage of the Indian Reorganization Act in 1934."[27] Now the goal was no longer to make Indians independent of federal oversight but to permanently enshrine that federal oversight. In the name of protecting Indians from rapacious white people, the federal government has made itself indispensable to Indians' daily economic lives.

Meanwhile, Indian land has become all but useless to Indians themselves. The patchwork left by Dawes and then the Indian Reorganization Act has meant that reservations include land owned by individual Indians, land owned by individual non-Indians, land owned in trust by individual Indians, and land owned in trust by the tribe. Any major development, whether real estate or natural resources, involves such complex negotiations that it's rarely worth the cost. Moreover, the federal government determined that land owned by individuals would be inherited equally by their children. It's possible for an individual to stipulate otherwise in a will, but as Small and plenty of other Indians have confirmed to me, wills weren't a part of traditional Indian culture, and few people ever wrote one.

The result is that "[t]hroughout Indian Country, most allotments have been subdivided and redivided so many times that they are worthless to the nominal owners," asserts Bordewich. He notes that in the early '90s, the chairman of the Omaha tribe was receiving "a total of $2.40 annually for his share of a family allotment whose ownership is splintered among more than two hundred heirs. Much land that is Indian-owned on paper has in fact become so fragmented that to be made economically viable at all, it has had to be leased out by the Bureau of Indian Affairs to white farmers and ranchers."[28]

In summary, the Dawes Act wasn't a good test of property rights, because Indians never had them.

In the past few decades, tribes in both the United States and Canada (which adopted a "reserve" system similar to our reservations) have attempted end-runs around this policy – some tribes will back mortgages for individuals, essentially putting up the tribal coffers as collateral on the loan. The effects are as predictable as they are disastrous, with tribes like the Kamloops in British Columbia paying millions of dollars a year to Canadian banks on behalf of their delinquent members.

Some tribes have made informal arrangements with banks – promising that if the banks are forced to foreclose, the tribe will help them find another buyer within the tribe so that they can recoup their losses.

When I ask Susan Woodrow, the assistant vice president and Helena branch executive of the Minneapolis Federal Reserve Bank, whether any of these strategies has been successful at improving rates of home-ownership or credit on the reservations, she tells me, "The short answer is no." Woodrow has spent much of the last 15 years helping tribes develop commercial law codes to encourage investment and private enterprise on the reservations. She describes some of the complex financial arrangements that tribe members have used to make mortgages possible, and they're nothing less than dizzying. As an example, Conrad Stewart tells me, "I had my dad give me a homesite lease on his property. That way the mortgage is not attached to the land; it's attached to the lease interest and based on the mortgage."

Homesite leases are typically entered into for a period of 25 years and then renewable for another 25. They're common on Indian land because of the difficulties of getting a regular mortgage, and the Bureau of Indian Affairs monitors them heavily. A group called PLACE Advocacy, based in Bozeman, Montana, tries to help Indians navigate these obstacles. Its website features a flowchart of 10 steps (not including any steps taken by the lender) that must be completed for such a lease to be approved. Perhaps the most noteworthy part of this document, though, is the helpful cartoon on the side explaining that leases can be agreed upon only for "fair market value." Fair market value "is the dollar value of a property based on a formal appraisal by the Office of Special Trustee (OST) in Billings."[29] A bureaucratic appraisal would obviously not be the definition of "fair market value" offered in most introductory economics textbooks. But on reservations, there can't be anything called "fair market value" when it comes to land, because none of the land is privately owned. "The American dream is homeownership," laments Stewart, "but that's not really possible here."

But there's more than homeownership at stake. American homes are one of the primary repositories of American wealth. And for those who want to start a business, they're one of the primary sources of start-up capital. But because Indians don't own their land – or, in most cases, their homes – they can't get credit, making it extraordinarily difficult for them to set up a small business. Stewart sums up the situation: "We are the highest regulated race in the world." Not only have individual American Indians been regulated into a kind of paralysis, larger economic projects on the reservation have all but stopped as a result of federal oversight.

If property rights on reservations were well defined, it would not only improve the housing stock and the general appearance of these communities but also significantly boost economic development. As Terry Anderson and Shawn Regan of the Property and Environmental Research Center wrote in 2013, "Crossing into reservations, especially in the West, reveals islands of poverty in a sea of wealth."[30] Crows and Northern Cheyennes sit on some of the largest oil, gas, and coal reserves in the country. Indian reservations, Anderson and Regan note, "contain almost 30% of the nation's coal reserves west of the Mississippi, 50% of potential uranium reserves, and 20% of known oil and gas reserves" – resources worth nearly $1.5 trillion, or $290,000 per tribal member. Tragically, "86% of Indian lands with energy or mineral potential remain undeveloped because of Federal control of reservations that keeps Indians from fully capitalizing on their natural resources if they desire."[31]

In order to tap into those reserves, Indians (whether the land is tribally held or individually held) must follow a 49-step process. These steps involve the Bureau of Land Management, the Department of the Interior, the Department of Justice, and the Commerce Department, explains an exasperated Stewart. And it can take months, if not years, for each step to be approved. Just to dig a hole, he says, requires a $6,500 up-front payment for an application for a permit to drill (APD).

Compare that, Stewart says, to the process just off the reservation, which requires about $125 and 15 minutes for the APD and then a mere five-step process for the permit to be approved. Stewart explains that although the tribe has had a coal mine since 1973, little progress has been made in getting resources out of the ground. The mine is the second largest in the nation, with 3 percent of the world's coal reserves, but it extracts only 5 million tons a year. A few miles off the reservation at Powder River, the yearly extraction is close to 120 million tons a year.

It's true that not every reservation is enthusiastic about the idea of natural resource development. The Northern Cheyenne are conducting a referendum on the issue, and though Ivan Small believes most tribe members would be in favor of it, he suggests that the tribal government is overly influenced by people concerned about the environmental impact. Winfield Russell, of the Northern Cheyenne tribal council, says he worries that development of the land "will undermine or destroy Native culture." Russell says he's not taking a position on the issue, but he sees a strong connection between the untouched land and the tribe's spiritual values. Unlike many other tribes, he says, "we're still strong here as far as our ceremonial culture and spirit on the reservation. We still have our covenant here."

Northern Cheyenne lands are almost entirely held in tribal trust, which means that no economic development on the reservation can happen without a vote of tribe members (in addition to all those bureaucratic steps at the federal level). This is why, for instance, the tribal two-year school, Chief Dull Knife College, can't expand its facility, even though enrollment has skyrocketed. "They will have to build up, not out," says Russell. "The college borders on a cemetery, and there is other land we can't go onto." The absurdity of adding additional stories to a building – this isn't New York City – on a reservation with hundreds of thousands of empty acres doesn't seem to strike anyone.

The Northern Cheyenne could sure use the money and jobs a coal mine like the Crows' would bring. The unemployment rate for the 8,000 tribe members who live on the reservation is more than 80 percent. And when I ask Russell how those members are employed, he offers the following list: "Tribal Health Services, the Bureau of Indian

Affairs, reservation schools, the roads department, the tribal court, tribal prosecution, our recovery center, and our tribal college."

That's it. He mentions not a single private enterprise. Russell laments that the most talented people on the reservation tend to leave. "On the outside, they have more pay, better benefits – that is where a person will go. That's what usually happens."

When I ask him what could be done to improve economic opportunity on the reservation, he tells me "more assistance from the federal government, helping the tribal government and financially assisting them and getting grants to the tribes." He also suggests the need for reforms at the Bureau of Indian Affairs. But nothing Russell suggests would do anything to encourage private enterprise. It would merely continue the same kind of dependent relationship the tribe has with the federal government right now.

To make matters worse, the federal government isn't even legally bound to deliver subsidies to Indians. In *Cherokee Nation v. Hitchcock* (1902) and *Lone Wolf v. Hitchcock* (1903), the Supreme Court ruled that treaties signed with Indians could be modified or terminated without Indians' consent. Indian leaders continue to cite the U.S. government's treaty obligations when explaining the need for the government to provide funding for education or health care. But the Snyder Act of 1921 allows the federal government to treat all tribes the same, regardless of the treaties those tribes signed. And as the Cato report notes, the Snyder Act "made Indian social programs subject to the same congressional spending adjustments as other programs."[32] Sadly, it seems that these spending adjustments are always going in one direction – up – and there's a general assumption that these programs will simply be permanent. But there's no guarantee.

To know just how much the economy on the reservation depends on public funds, one need only learn the effects that the federal government shutdown in the fall of 2013 had on Indian reservations. Take the Crow tribe. Some 364 Crow members, more than a third of the tribe's workforce, were furloughed. A bus service, the only way some Crows are able to travel across their 2.3-million-acre reservation, was shuttered. A home health care program for sick tribal members was suspended.[33]

The Yurok tribe in Northern California relies almost solely on federal financing to operate. Its reservation has an 80 percent unemployment rate. As a result of the shutdown, the tribe furloughed 60 of its 310 employees, closed its child care center, and halted emergency financial assistance to low-income and older members. Financing for a program that ensures clean drinking water on the reservation ran low.[34]

These tribes are so dependent on the federal government that without money from the Bureau of Indian Affairs, their economic activity comes to a complete halt and their members may not have access to clean drinking water.

Despite the vast amount of federal money that does usually flow to these communities, there's little accountability. Though there were some reforms in the 1970s, many tribal governments are rife with corruption. And the lack of a private economy makes things worse. If all jobs are government jobs, then they become all the more important as prizes to be given to supporters or simply to extended family.

Still, in every community I visited, a few people like Ivan Small understood that no amount of federal funds was going to stop the poverty and dysfunction. What they longed for wasn't more money. They didn't care for more apologies or hand-wringing from white folks in Washington. What they wanted was what Senator Dawes once promised their people – emancipation.

The problem is the same in Canada, says Manny Jules, one of the leaders of the Kamloops band in the province of British Columbia: First Nations (as Canadian Aboriginals are called) don't have real property rights. And property rights, he says, "are human rights." Of course, the notion that Indians believe in property rights is contrary to everything that you hear about Aboriginal Peoples, he notes.

A small, gray-haired man with a warm smile, Jules went to art school when he was younger, hoping to become a sculptor. But he put that pursuit aside to assume a leadership role, first as a councilor of the Kamloops band, then as its chief and one of the cofounders of the Shuswap tribal council, of which the Kamloops band is a part.

The city of Kamloops (2011 population: 85,678) enjoys a gorgeous setting. In the same hotel I stay at are hikers, mountain bikers, and nature lovers. In the heart of Kamloops is the confluence of the North and South Thompson Rivers – the former flowing from the Thompson Glacier at the foot of the Caribou Mountains, the latter coming from Little Shuswap Lake (which, at 7 miles long and 5 miles wide, is not so little). In the summer, Canadian and international travelers eager to experience the region's natural beauty come in busloads. The days are hot and dry, but in the evenings, when the temperature cools down, families gather at the well-kept public beaches and parks along the rivers.

There are a few expensive restaurants in Kamloops whose menus emphasize "local ingredients," but mostly the city has the feel of a middle-class oasis where people have found the right balance of work and play. Railway lines meet here, so the region is a hub of economic activity. There are coal mines and copper mines. Natural resources are plentiful.

But if you want to see how the land question affects members of First Nations, drive at night to the top of one of the peaks overlooking the city. On one side of the river, there are lights everywhere – apartment buildings, homes, businesses, and hotels. On the other side – the land held by Jules's band – there's mostly darkness. It's not quite as stark as the difference between North and South Korea in satellite images, but it comes remarkably close.

The first thing you notice when you drive to the other side of the river is the waterfront. Right on the edge of the rivers is a trailer park with hundreds of homes so close together they might as well be on top of one another. A little ways back from that are some lumberyards and car dealerships interspersed with small homes, many of which are badly in need of repair.

Much of this part of town has a feel of impermanence to it. And that's no accident, explains André Le Dressay of Fiscal Realities Economists, a group that conducts economic research and analysis, develops innovative solutions, and advises and advocates for public, First Nation, and private sector clients. In the Kamloops area, Le Dressay estimates that a First Nation member-owned home is worth about $\frac{1}{20}$th what it's worth off reserve. "These are classic economic results."

"You don't see big permanent structure leases for less than 15 years," Le Dressay tells me as we drive around the Indian side of the water. On the side that's not a reserve, homes sell for more than half a million dollars, but here the most profit to be made off the land is from a trailer park. Since the band has no money, they're unable to create the public parks and other facilities you see on the other side of Kamloops. They're barely able to keep up with the projects they do oversee. The cemetery holds victims of the 1860 smallpox epidemic as well as veterans of the World Wars, Korea, and Vietnam, but it looks overgrown. The local Catholic church is undergoing a much-needed renovation, but the houses around it are falling apart.

In another attempt to work around the land problem, some First Nations have arrangements whereby a bank will give band members a mortgage, but if the members default, the band itself is on the hook for the money. The results are predictable: the Kamloops band is paying more than $2 million a year in arrears. And it's not only the mortgage payments that are the problem, it's the upkeep. Le Dressay tells me that the "average lifespan of a tribal home is 15 years." That is, homes are so poorly cared for that they need to be completely demolished and rebuilt after only 15 years.

There's one large gated community on the Indian side of the river. The tribe came to a complex agreement with a developer for a 99-year lease on the land. The community has its own restaurant and golf course, and plenty of non-Indians have purchased homes here.

But for every successful development project, there are several others that have fallen through. Twenty years ago, a plan for a big hotel and residential development brought together seven or eight landowners, Le Dressay recalls. "But it took so long to get the regulatory approvals and the environmental approvals that the lenders got nervous. One of the front men eventually committed suicide because of all the pressure. It never took off." Studies by Fiscal Realities have found that development on the Indian side of the river takes, on average, four to six times longer than development on land off the reserve.[35]

Jules supports a parliamentary proposal, the First Nations Property Ownership Act, which would address this problem by allowing First Nations to have title to their own lands instead of having the Canadian federal government hold those lands in trust. But "one of the biggest challenges we face in convincing people about [the First Nations Property Ownership Act] is mythology," says Le Dressay. "The popular understanding of indigenous culture is that it's almost like there was a socialist utopia for millennia." But such a utopia never existed. As Le Dressay notes, "In any other circumstances such a society would have been impossible – unless you consider North Korea a success story." But people continue to impose this history on First Nations, as if they're exceptions to human nature.

A lot of the literature on First Nations' history and traditions was written in the 1960s and 1970s – a time when environmentalism and socialism were surging in the West. More was contributed in the 1980s, a time of political correctness, when scholars pushed the notion that traditional cultures were far ahead of the dominant Western one because of their communalist impulses.

After engaging in extensive research on his own communities and others in Canada, the United States, and Mexico, Jules has come to the conclusion that this is all bunk. "Property rights are part of indigenous culture," he tells me in no uncertain terms. As he explains, "In my community, we have some of the oldest pit house sites." Pit houses were permanent structures requiring considerable time and resources to build. "They were nice and toasty warm in the winter. In the summer we went out and gathered salmon, berries, wild vegetables, and hunted game. In the winter we came back to settled villages. There is no way we would have left and come back to allow some other family to live in our pit house."

And yet political leaders and educators continue to offer sentimental myths in place of this history. Michelle Obama recently told a gathering of Native American youth, "Long before the United States was even an idea, your ancestors were harvesting the crops that would feed the world for centuries to come" and "Today on issues like conservation and climate change, we are finally beginning to embrace the wisdom of your ancestors."[36]

Mrs. Obama hasn't discovered some ancient Indian text that predicted the melting of the glaciers. And there's little evidence that Indians had any fundamentally different understanding of the environment than any other people on Earth. Which is to say, when resources were scarce, Natives worked to conserve them. When resources weren't scarce, they didn't.

Take, for instance, the oft-repeated notion that Indians would "use every part of the animal" – because of their concern for nature and their desire not to waste its treasures. History doesn't back that up. In a 2002 article called "Buffaloed: The Myth and Reality of Bison in America," historian Larry Schweikart notes that some Indian tribes cleared large amounts of forest with "controlled burns" for hunting purposes. They would divert game into small, unburned areas to make it easier to hunt the animals.[37]

As if that weren't bad enough from an "environmental" perspective, Schweikart says, the intentional fires "often got out of control, and without modern firefighting equipment, flashed through forests, destroying everything in their path. Deer, beaver and birds of all sorts were already on a trajectory to extinction in some areas, because over and above the hunting done by Indians, natural predators and disasters thinned herds." Other hunting methods included the "buffalo jump," in which a man would drive an entire herd over a cliff. As Schweikart notes, this "led to horrible waste and inefficient use of resources." When buffalo were plentiful, they were hunted without regard to waste. When their numbers dwindled, things changed.[38]

To the extent that Native Americans of old cared about conservation, it was when they owned things. Jules notes that the same is true of the Natives who lived in Canada, saying, "The teepees were owned by individual women." He leans in to emphasize the point. "The concept that we never had private property has been foisted upon us." It's interesting that in revisionist academics' attempts to suggest that First Nations are more advanced due to their communal attitudes, they've actually "reinforced the notion that we are not as advanced as somebody else, as Western culture."

Jules believes that the time for passively accepting the status quo is over. During three decades of involvement in tribal leadership, he has tried to significantly alter federal policy toward Indians, creating greater political and economic autonomy for First Nations. He has worked with other leaders to develop political clout, so that the Canadian government can't ignore them.

Self-sufficiency has become Jules's mantra for the Kamloops band and for all the First Nations of Canada. He seems to have the right combination of experience and optimism to make changes happen in his community. Jules's father, a logger and a cowboy who could, according to Jules, "ride from the time he could walk," set up the first industrial park on a Canadian reserve. In 1963, 14 businesses opened there, but the logistical problems of doing business on the reserve immediately became obvious: Jules's father had a tough time getting anyone to plow the roads in winter. The province claimed that snow removal was the federal government's responsibility – because the reserve was federal land – but the federal government said it was the province's responsibility because the province collected taxes on the land.[39] This controversy led to a decades-long fight with the Canadian government – specifically over issues of taxation, but more broadly about political and economic autonomy for First Nations.

In 1988, thanks to Jules's leadership in calling for reform, Parliament passed "The Kamloops Amendment," the first-ever First Nation–led change to the Indian Act. The Indian Act has regulated the 614

First Nation bands in Canada ever since it was passed in 1876. The Kamloops Amendment established the power of governments of First Nations to levy property taxes on reserves, including taxes on lease-hold developments like the industrial park Jules's father helped launch. It also allowed governments of First Nations to set land aside for leasing and economic development without that land losing its reserve status. This was the first step in gaining more fiscal and political autonomy for First Nations.

The First Nations Property Ownership Act would create the legal framework for individual members of First Nations to access capital through secure property rights. This legislation would make First Nations like small provinces or cities. Just as land belongs to the city of Quebec even though residents of the city can buy and sell it among themselves, so people in the Kamloops band would be able to have individual title to their land (to do with as they wish); at the same time, the land would be taxed and its public facilities would be maintained by the band.

The First Nations Property Ownership Act could be a political and economic game-changer for Aboriginal Peoples. But to understand why, it's necessary to know more about the history of First Nations in Canada, as well as the ways in which the Canadian "reserve system" is different from the U.S. reservation system.

The Canadian and American systems have common origins in the Royal Proclamation of 1763. As Kathy Brock wrote in her contribution to *Canada and the United States: Differences That Count*, "Embedded in the [British] proclamation is an ambivalence that gave rise to two very different histories of Aboriginal governance in Canada and the United States. On the one hand, the proclamation recognized that Indian nations were independent and should be dealt with through treaties by central authorities. The document established the basis of treaty and reservation land systems, and provided a basis for current land claims. On the other hand, the proclamation confirmed that Indian tribes possessed a limited sovereignty and were subject to British rule. Thus, they were not seen as equal to European nations, and limits were imposed on their actions when practically possible."[40]

Although Brock, a professor in the School of Policy Studies and Department of Political Studies at Queen's University, argues that the U.S. government has largely allowed tribes to govern themselves – for better or for worse – as long as they stay within their reservation borders and live without any property rights – the Canadian policy has been characterized by micromanagement of tribal affairs. In addition to the forced assimilation carried out by the residential schooling programs (to be covered in chapter 4), which also existed in the United States, but to a much smaller extent, Brock says, "almost every conceivable facet of First Nation life and culture was subject to scrutiny and regulation by Indian Affairs officials."[41] Although Indian agents were largely absent from American reservations after the first decade of the 20th century, Indian agents (also known as superintendents) weren't removed from Canadian reserves until 1975, and then it was because members of First Nations "occupied" these offices and kicked them out.

Remarkably, the Canadian government even determines who is and who isn't a member of a First Nation. If your bloodline is too diluted due to intermarriage, Ottawa will not regard you as Indian. (In America, as long as a person is claimed by an officially recognized tribe, he or she is treated as American Indian.)

Ironically, the fact that so much power rests with the federal government means that significant policy changes have been much more forthcoming in Canada than in the United States. These shifts began in the 1960s, Brock explains to me, "as part of dialogue around the world about the importance of self-government." In 1973, the Canadian Supreme Court recognized Aboriginal title to the land in *Calder v. British Columbia*.

The landmark *Calder* case clarified matters only so much, though. Three of the justices claimed that Indian title to the land existed at one point but had been extinguished by virtue of the government's exercise of control over the lands. Which is to say that since the Canadian government had been in charge of their lands for so long, Indians could no longer claim title. The other three justices said more evidence had to be presented to show that the title was extinguished.

Even though the practical results of *Calder* were unclear, says Brock, "it proved to be a catalyst." A lot of administrative arrangements were transferred to Indian bands. The opening up of oil and gas resources in western Canada brought many of these issues of economic independence to a head. In 1982, when the Canadian government "patriated" the constitution from Britain, it also adopted a charter of rights, which included a section on Aboriginal land and titles. Prior to this, the Canadian constitution was technically part of British law. This new stage of Canadian law provided an opportunity to alter and clarify the Canadian federal government's relationship with First Nations.

Starting in 1984, a series of court decisions advanced the claims and rights of First Nations. There were a number of talks between the prime minister, leaders of First Nations, and provincial leaders to try to define Aboriginal rights. Talks broke down in 1987, with no clear definition emerging, but as Brock tells me, "Aboriginals were established as the rightful leaders for the community."

Much of the impetus for these court decisions and political negotiations came from the province of British Columbia. In part, this was because so many British Columbian tribes never signed official treaties with the colonial British or French government, unlike tribes in the eastern parts of Canada. And so their relationship with the Canadian government was even more ambiguous than that of their peers to the east. With the wealth of natural resources up for grabs in British Columbia, the area was ripe for litigation.

The only bands in British Columbia that did have agreements with the former British government were the groups on the southern part of Vancouver Island that had signed the Douglas Treaties. Between 1850 and 1864, Sir James Douglas served as representative of Hudson's Bay Company and then as governor of Vancouver Island and British

Columbia. He was primarily interested in maintaining a peaceable environment for trading and, as such, sought to purchase land from the First Nations in the area.

Douglas seemed to recognize that Indians thought of the land as their own – not as belonging to everyone or to the gods or Nature, broadly speaking, as is often assumed. On March 25, 1861, Douglas wrote to the Duke of Newcastle, who was then secretary of state for the Canadian colonies, "praying for the aid of Her Majesty's Government in extinguishing the Indian title to the public lands in this Colony." He wanted money to pay the Indians for their land, arguing that the natives had "distinct ideas of property in land, and mutually recognize[d] their several exclusive rights in certain districts."[42] The First Nations varied in size, and some of them were effectively extended families, whereas others divided up their land among different families within the band. The point is this: even before Europeans arrived, the First Nations in the area had divided the land among themselves and didn't think of it as collectively held or, alternatively, unowned.

Douglas warned that failure to extinguish title and "the occupation of such portions of the Colony by white settlers, unless with the full consent of the proprietary tribes," would be perceived "as national wrongs, engender feelings of irritation against the settlers, and endanger the peace of the country." As the authors of a recent paper prepared for the Union of British Columbia Indian Chiefs explain, "Douglas estimated that it would cost 3,000 pounds sterling to extinguish title to the remaining settled districts of the Colony: He asked that the British Government extend a loan in the form of a grant to be repaid from the proceeds of consequent sale of public lands in the Colony."[43]

The British government turned him down, and, as a result, most of the First Nations in British Columbia remained without treaties right up until recent times. A new treaty process was begun in 1993, under which tribes were supposed to give up their claims to certain land and occupy others in return for compensation. About a third of the tribes in British Columbia have begun the process, but not much progress has been made.[44]

And the future of such negotiations doesn't look promising. According to Mark Milke, the author of a report for the Fraser Institute, a Canadian think tank, "After 15 years of negotiation with BC Indian bands at a cost of more than $1.1 billion, the province has only eight treaties that have either been passed, initialled or are in the final negotiating stage."[45] The report is titled *Incomplete, Illiberal, and Expensive: A Review of 15 Years of Treaty Negotiations in British Columbia and Proposals for Reform*, and Milke notes that "government representatives have taken negotiating positions that will lead to never-ending discussions and the creation of massive legal and regulatory bodies to support ongoing consultation. Effectively, this means the treaty process never ends."[46]

Meanwhile the legal question of "Aboriginal title" is working its way through the courts as well: do First Nations have any claim to land that is *not* part of their reserves? After *Calder*, cases in 1984 and 1997 and most recently in 2014 expanded and solidified Aboriginal title as a concept in Canadian law.

Indeed, in 2014, in *Tsilhqot'in Nation v. British Columbia*, the Supreme Court granted title to First Nations on land that was off of their reserves. The Tsilhqot'in claimed that the government of British Columbia didn't have the right to grant a commercial logging license on land that First Nations had occupied continuously for hundreds of years. And the court agreed.

Written by Chief Justice Beverley McLachlin, the unanimous ruling says that Aboriginal title "flows from occupation in the sense of regular and exclusive use of land.... Occupation sufficient to ground aboriginal title is not confined to specific sites of settlement, but extends to tracts of land that were regularly used for hunting, fishing or otherwise exploiting resources and over which the group exercised effective control at the time of assertion of European sovereignty."[47]

When I visited Kamloops several weeks after this decision was handed down, leaders of First Nations, including Manny Jules, were working furiously to come up with their response to this decision. How would it affect their willingness to participate in the treaty process? Would it change people's support for the First Nations Property Ownership Act? If millions of acres of land were now in play, should First Nations really focus their efforts on gaining clearer title only to land on the reserves?

There was a great deal of disagreement among the leaders I spoke with about exactly what this decision would mean. In principle, it could mean that First Nations could claim the entire city of Kamloops, one of the top 50 metropolitan areas in the country. Would they be compensated by the tens of thousands of residents and businesses occupying land that First Nations once used for hunting? And which bands could rightly claim title? Some bands have claimed overlapping lands. Hunting lands in particular were hard to demarcate.

Although some Canadian Indians are hopeful that a claim to Aboriginal title will expand their claims on the land, others are concerned that this will only inject more uncertainty into the land question, which is the last thing that those interested in economic growth want to see. Though these disputes over land ownership and political autonomy have been around for more than a century, leaders of First Nations have good reason to want to see a resolution to these matters sooner rather than later. They know from numerous investors that the only way more money will flow to First Nations is if there's some certainty about who owns and who's responsible for the land on and off the reserves.

In their introduction to the book *Beyond the Indian Act*, Tom Flanagan, Christopher Alcantara, and André Le Dressay lay out the problems succinctly: "Aboriginal people are the least prosperous demographic group in Canada. In life expectancy, income, unemployment, welfare dependency, educational attainment, and quality of housing, the pattern is the same: aboriginal people trail other Canadians. And within the category of aboriginal people, another pattern also stands out: First Nations (status Indians) do worse than Métis and non-status Indians; while among First Nations, those living on-reserve do worse than those living off-reserve." The future seems pretty bleak too. As the authors note, "These patterns have been more or less stable for decades. Aboriginal people and First Nations are progressing on most indicators compared to other Canadians, but the progress is painfully slow, and it will take centuries to achieve parity at these rates of change."[48]

It's worth noting the similarity of this situation with that of tribes in the United States. Observers often say that Indians are more visible in Canada because other racial minorities make up a smaller proportion of Canada's population than America's. In other words, the problems of blacks and Hispanics overshadow the problems of Indians in the United States.

But the land problems and the resulting government policies are at the heart of why both American and Canadian Indians are experiencing so many economic and social problems.

The reserve lands in Canada don't have the "patchworking" problem that resulted from the policy of allotment in the United States. In Canada, bands themselves (as opposed to individual Indians) collectively hold much more of the reserve lands than is the case in America. But Canadian Indians still have the same underlying problem. First Nations technically have title to the land, but it can only be "alienated" – that is, it can only be sold – through the federal government, and, as Brock told me, "the Crown has a fiduciary duty to make sure the land fetches a fair price."

But now the question is how to move forward. The first priority, Jules says, is to change or repeal the Indian Act. The Indian Act "freezes things in place," notes Jules. It was "written when we were a dying people." But if there's to be change in policy at the federal level, First Nations need to be prepared to take over certain aspects of their own governance. If First Nations are eventually to be treated as another province – one possible outcome here – what tasks are they willing and able to take on?

The leaders of tribes in British Columbia commissioned a report looking at 200 different areas of governance. "We don't want our own postal service or our own standing army," says Jules. But they do want more responsibility for taxation and local services, including utilities and education.

One advantage that First Nations have over their American brethren is that they're a significant political force. According to Canada's 2006 census, Aboriginal Peoples compose about 3.6 percent of the Canadian population. Compare this proportion with only 1.7 percent in the United States.[49] Because of their geographic distribution, Canadian Indians have significantly more political power as well. Indian politicians not only have been elected to Parliament but also hold the majority of elected seats in two provincial legislatures. American Indians, by contrast, have amassed no such power. And although they may be influential in, say, the election of a legislator from South Dakota, they're not going to be able to sway many votes in Washington.

Also, the population of First Nations is growing rapidly. According to official estimates, between 1971 and 2011, it grew by 487 percent, while the total Canadian population grew by 52 percent. Although some of that growth is attributable to a greater number of people claiming Aboriginal ancestry, it's true that the birth rate among Aboriginal Peoples is higher than among the rest of the population. According to the Canadian government, "Amongst the Aboriginal population, 46% of individuals are under age 25, compared to 29% for the rest of the Canadian population."[50]

These numbers have started to make political leaders pay attention. In a book called *Time Bomb*, Doug Bland, former chair of Defence Management Studies at Queen's University, argues that the conditions are ripe for an uprising by First Nations, whose economic and political aspirations have been stifled for so long. Bland foresees the potential shutdown of major means of transportation by protests and civil unrest. He told the *Ottawa Citizen* that he was "not predicting a revolution or an armed uprising." But because the population of First

Nations is disproportionately young and "concentrated in areas critically important to Canada's resource industries and transportation infrastructure," he said he sees the potential for a real standoff of some sort. He warns that a "confrontation" could occur if Canadian and First Nation leaders can't solve some of their conflicts.[51]

But the difficulties in resolving these conflicts stem from more than intransigence on the part of the Canadian government. Because Canadian bands operate independently – some have fewer than 100 members – it can be very hard to get any kind of broad agreement among First Nations when lobbying for a particular policy.

Indeed, because some bands may not want these property rights, one selling point of the First Nations Property Ownership Act (Jules and his allies emphasize this repeatedly) is that any band can choose not to "opt in" to the legislation. Every band should at least have the *opportunity* to introduce property rights, however.

For all the concern about an imminent revolution on the part of First Nations and the groundbreaking high court decisions that have been handed down, not much has really changed on the reserves. Mike Lebourdais, the chief of the Whispering Pines/Clinton band, who live a couple of hours from Kamloops, tells me that the federal government has made it impossible for bands to improve their situation economically. The best advice he can give his children and the children of others in his band is to get an education and leave, and so his band spends more than most on education. They not only pay for primary and secondary education but also spend almost $300,000 a year to help pay for postsecondary education. A number of times, I hear from leaders of First Nations that education is "the one thing the government can't take away from you."

The entire Whispering Pines band – today about 56 members – moved to Whispering Pines only in 1972. Their traditional lands are farther north, but when the government started developing hydroelectric power there, a transmission system was built right through the band's land. The Ministry of Indian Affairs "is never proactive," says Lebourdais, but once it recognized the land was "unlivable," the ministry gave Whispering Pines a new reserve.

As I drive to Whispering Pines from Kamloops, it's very easy to see the borders between band land and privately owned land, even without crossing the Thompson Rivers. The farmland that seems to speed by my window goes from lush green to brown and then back again.

That's because, for one thing, band members couldn't get a bank loan for an irrigation system. "We don't have a balance sheet," Lebourdais explains. "We have an expense statement, but we don't have a balance sheet. So you're going to spend $15,000 or $18,000 a year on electricity for property that doesn't exist on paper. It exists in real life – you can touch it, feel it – but it doesn't mean anything to a banker unless you can describe it legally." And the entire system makes no sense to a banker because you're trying to irrigate land you don't actually own. Which is why, says Lebourdais, "everything is cash on the reserve."

The fact that the land is held in trust by the Canadian government restricts the economy on the reserve to cash or barter, forcing the Whispering Pines band to live in a kind of preindustrial society.

To illustrate this point, Ed Lebourdais, Mike's brother, describes a meeting he had recently with the minister of Indian affairs (known officially now as the minister of Aboriginal affairs and northern development). "We're all equals," the minister told him. To which Ed said:

"No, we're not."

He said, "We're all Canadians."

I said, "No. No. Your house is worth something. Mine's not. And if you don't believe me, let's trade houses." You could hear a pin drop in that office, because nobody wanted to say anything. I smiled at him and he smiled back, and I said, "Exactly. So don't sit there and tell me we're equals." When he holds all the cards, has all the finances, has all the money, all the jurisdiction, all the authority, and none of the accountability.

Indian property isn't easily transferable to other Indians either. The Indian Act makes it very difficult for Indians to will their homes to their children. And so, more often than not, after the death of its owner, a home is simply auctioned off to the highest bidder.

Take the situation of Deana Crawford. About 15 years ago, Deana, who is not Indian, married a member of the Whispering Pines band. She and her husband had two children and then he left her. Every month, she pays rent on the home, which is located on land owned by the band. But no matter how much she pays, she's no closer to owning the home. Even though her children are members of the band, she isn't allowed to own band land. She can never get a mortgage for the land. And she can't leave it to her children.

Lebourdais has encouraged his small band to be as entrepreneurial as possible given the circumstances. Within the band, a group of firefighters contract with the provincial government to combat forest fires in other parts of British Columbia and other parts of Canada as well. It's a business that doesn't require any land, so it's more feasible than many other enterprises, though it did require the purchase of some equipment.

Lebourdais is disdainful of the dependence on government that many bands seem to have developed. The government sends Lebourdais money each month for what's called Social Assistance. But Lebourdais says he refuses to sign those checks over to members of his band unless they can prove that they're physically incapable of working. "I'll probably get in trouble for this, but I don't care," he tells me.

Lebourdais is adamant: "There is no reason for an 18-year-old person to be on welfare. No good reason, anyway. You've got both arms, both legs, you got a dog with you for your eyesight. We'll get you a job, whether it's washing cars or washing dishes. If you think you're worth more than that, go apply yourself, because I'm not going to cut you a check." Lebourdais says people are better off this way – "you have better self-esteem, better values, better thoughts, when you have a real paycheck."

Lebourdais sees the alternative everywhere he looks. In the Kamloops band, he says, "there are families that think, 'The government owes me a house, so I'm not paying for this one.'" They don't pay their mortgages or take care of their homes because they think that's the band's responsibility. Lebourdais doesn't want that to happen to Whispering Pines.

Keith Matthew, former chief of the Simpcw band, which, like Kamloops, is part of the Shuswap Nation, recalls that when he was growing up "there wasn't really much of an economy at all" on his reserve. "We still had an Indian agent," he tells me, referring to the person sent by the Ministry of Indian Affairs to oversee all the activities of the reserve. In 1975, Matthew's father was one of the band members who occupied the Indian agent's office. "We were kicking the Indian agent out of our lives on an everyday basis," Matthew says of the occupation, after which money began to flow from the federal government directly to the band. "That was an important turning point in our history."

That was also the time at which the residential school was closed down. Matthew went to a local school nearby. Today, he says proudly, "My community is one of the highest educated ones in Canada per capita. We have our first medical doctor. We have people training to be lawyers. We have lots of teachers." Unfortunately, says Matthew, because of the constraints of the Indian Act, "it's tough to build an economy on the reserve ... and two-thirds of the Simpcw live off reserve." But like the Kamloops band, their neighbors 50 miles to the south, the Simpcw are trying to build up the infrastructure so that once they're given more economic and political autonomy they'll be poised to take control.

Because the Simpcw live in a very rural area, there's a limit to how much they'll be able to collect in property taxes, but they've started a group of band-owned companies in order to supplement their reserves. There's a power line construction company and an environmental consulting company, for instance.

And ten years ago, the Simpcw launched a partnership with a heli-skiing company. For $1,500, thrill-seekers can go to the top of a mountain in a helicopter and then ski down. "It's a very high-end clientele," says Matthew. But the deal almost didn't happen, because the band had difficulty coming up with its portion of the start-up money. "We found out in a hurry that we're a bad risk." They had no collateral to put down. But in 2003, there was a huge fire in the valley near their reserve. They bid on a job to remove all the salvage wood. They sold the wood and then used that money to invest in the heli-skiing venture.

There are many such opportunities for bands to make money from tourism, if only they can find the start-up capital. I meet Felix Arnouse, chief of the Little Shuswap band, at the Quaaout Lodge at Talking Rock Golf Course. Interest in building a resort on this lake began in the 1970s after the local Indian Affairs office was shut down. But the hotel wasn't actually opened until 1990, Arnouse recalls.

Although financing the project was the biggest hurdle, many band members were opposed to getting involved in any kind of business venture, believing that they'd inevitably get the short end of the stick from non-Indian partners. And many, says Arnouse, "still think it's a bad idea." Like Indian casinos in the United States, the Quaaout Lodge manages to provide jobs for band members who want them, but there's still not much in the way of private enterprise here.

Some band members still live in poverty, and many struggle with drug and alcohol addiction, Arnouse tells me. There are fights over who should pay the mortgages on individual band members' homes. Arnouse, himself a recovering alcoholic, says that he sees the cycle over and over. "They drink and party and end up fighting. It's a big thing in Native culture." Some fights can lead to years of animosity, which spill over into the governance of the nation. Band members have made some reforms in tribal governance – such as instituting four-year terms for the chief – that will give businesses that work with them a sense of certainty about the future. But a lot of decisions are clearly driven by family politics.

The band did manage to get a loan from the federal government to build the resort, but band members did a lot of the actual construction. Despite the lodge's success, Arnouse says they've had to be very careful about any expansion plans because it's still very hard for them to get credit.

Arnouse is a supporter of the property rights legislation, but some of his band members, not to mention other band leaders, are opposed to it. But because the legislation doesn't bind First Nations to adopt the policies, Arnouse and Lebourdais seem confident that Parliament will pass the First Nations Property Ownership Act within the next couple of years. Regardless of which political party is in power, Lebourdais believes there'll be enough support for it. "This isn't my first rodeo," he assures me.

The biggest opposition, Lebourdais says, has come from other First Nations. "They think that white people are going to buy up the reserves," he tells me. But under the terms of the act, the land would remain part of the reserve, just as other land might remain part of a city. And there's something else, says Lebourdais: Aboriginal people in Canada "think property ownership is a white thing." He worries that they really don't understand their own history. "They've come to think that reserves are the way it was."

But Lebourdais has educated himself about the way things were. In the summer of 1910, Prime Minister Sir Wilfrid Laurier went on a tour of Canada. On August 25, he was met in Kamloops by a delegation of chiefs from the Secwépemc, Nlaka'pamux, and Syilx nations, who offered him a history of how their people had lived before whites came to their territory and what had happened since their first encounters a century earlier.

When they first came among us there were only Indians here. They found the people of each tribe supreme in their own territory, and having tribal boundaries known and recognized by all. The country of each tribe was just the same as a very large farm or ranch (belonging to all the people of the tribe) from which they gathered their food and clothing, etc., fish which they got in plenty for food, grass and vegetation on which their horses grazed and the game lived, and much of which furnished materials for manufactures, etc., stone which furnished pipes, utensils, and tools, etc., trees which furnished firewood, materials for houses and utensils, plants, roots, seeds, nuts and berries which grew abundantly and were gathered in their season just the same as the crops on a ranch, and used for food; minerals, shells, etc., which were used for ornament and for plants, etc., water which was free to all.[52]

The purpose of this letter to Laurier was to complain about the reserve system – that is, the chiefs noted that they had been promised sufficient land to continue their farming and ranching activities, as well as access to water sources and the ability to travel freely off the reserve. White settlers had gone back on these promises, as occurred across much of the American and Canadian West. But in their hopes to get Laurier to intervene on their behalf, the chiefs invoked their own history of property rights.

As the authors of *Beyond the Indian Act* write, "the historical evidence shows that the aboriginal peoples of North America are like all other human beings. They claim territories as collectivities but have no particular aversion to private property in the hands of families and individuals. Unless they are prevented by the *force majeure* of government, they change with the times and are willing to adopt whatever institutions of property are most economically efficient for the world in which they live."[53]

It's astonishing just how much First Nations have managed to accomplish while living within the confines of the Indian Act. After getting the heli-skiing venture off the ground, the Simpcw worked to ensure that they had more of a say in other sorts of development going on around them.

In 2004, the Canadian Supreme Court ruled that the Crown had a "duty to consult" with Aboriginal Peoples before developing land on which they may have claims, even if those claims are unproven. In reaction to this decision, Matthew and his colleagues developed a "consultation accommodation framework," which they now present to companies interested in doing business on their territory (both on and off reserve). "In the past, companies have just treated us as a second thought, so they would get a license to do business on the territories without telling us what they wanted to do." Now, the Simpcw not only get some of the revenues from projects with companies like BC Hydro but also ensure that companies mitigate the environmental impacts of the projects and reserve a certain number of jobs for members of the band. A lot of Simpcw have gained experience from these ventures, says Matthew, experience that they've been able to put to use on other projects. The arrangement and its benefits are similar to the ones that the Seneca Nation has been able to gain in upstate New York by creating construction firms that contract with the federal government.

In a 2007 agreement with Kinder Morgan Canada, Matthew says, the Simpcw were given contracting agreements. They provided emergency flagging crews for construction workers, for instance. This has led to other opportunities, such as driving ambulances. Now, even when companies like these aren't working on Aboriginal lands, they hire Simpcw people with this kind of experience to help.

These frameworks are frankly not the ideal means of economic growth. Many companies probably see them as an elaborate shakedown mechanism, but at least the firms are getting some "certainty" out of the agreement. Matthew doesn't see these agreements as the endgame for his band, either. He calls these projects "low-hanging fruit" that his people can pick while waiting for some kind of reform to come out of Ottawa.

He complains that anything from registering a lease to dealing with a will can take decades on the reserve. "My father passed away intestate and it took 20 years to settle the land issue," Matthew says. "When you have archaic clauses that govern how you do business on a reserve, there is virtually no opportunity for the creation of our own local economy."

When I ask Matthew what could possibly take 20 years for the approval of his father's will by the Canadian government, he answers, "I don't know; I'm not a bureaucrat. I don't know anyone who works in Indian Land Management." Of course, one problem is that federal bureaucrats are far removed from what's happening on the ground with these bands. But another is what Matthew refers to as the "cover your ass policy," which simply means, as he says, "They're not going to risk it."

Risk what?

Because the land is held in trust and because the government has a "fiduciary responsibility" to protect the interests of First Nations, the Canadian government is essentially liable if anything goes wrong. For instance, if a band builds a copper mine on reserve lands and an accident results in some kind of environmental contamination, the Canadian government is responsible for the consequences. As Matthew notes, the band could sue Ottawa for allowing the mine to be built. Under this system, First Nations are essentially denied the chance to take responsibility for their own future. "In the eyes of the federal government," Matthew notes, "as a Status Indian I am still a child."

This is a theme I hear again and again from the chiefs. As Jules says, "In Canada, there are three types of individuals not allowed to own property – kids, the mentally incompetent, and Indians living on reserves." Fixing this problem, he says, is a matter of "social justice." Indians need to be able "to participate in the economy." It's not enough to get a few jobs out of a big natural resources project. It's not enough to be able to conduct a gaming operation. "We need a diverse economy."

But Jules worries that his people have been living in a state of dependency for so long that they'll need to train themselves to take responsibility again. He tells me that he was recently at a meeting of Saskatchewan chiefs discussing the problem of crack cocaine in their communities. He relates one chief's proposed solution: "We need a billboard outside the communities that says 'don't bring drugs here.'" Jules sighs. "They think the problem is people outside bringing it in. The problem is in our community."

When Jules looks around at the different pathologies affecting First Nations – from low levels of education to drug abuse to poverty to domestic violence – he says, "We have ingrained in us the mentality that it's someone else's responsibility. We have seen a complete abdication." For things to get better, he says, "The leadership has to come from us."

In his 2010 best seller *Empire of the Summer Moon*, journalist S. C. Gwynne recounts the remarkable story of Quanah Parker, a Comanche born around 1849. Quanah's father, Peta Nocona, was a Comanche chief; his mother, Cynthia Parker, was white. She had been kidnapped at age nine and assimilated into the tribe. After Quanah's father was killed in battle with Texas Rangers, his mother was taken away to live with her white relatives. But Quanah emerged from the ordeal a leader of his people, trying to improve their situation even as they were placed on reservations and forced to sell their land under the policy of allotment. Quanah negotiated with the U.S. government for more land and more money. He bought and sold cattle, he bought and sold land, and he sold protection for whites who wanted to move their cattle across Indian lands.

Quanah became quite wealthy and remained enormously generous to his people, dying with almost nothing to his name. Though Gwynne claims that "the first generations of Comanches in captivity never really understood the concept of wealth, of private property," Quanah clearly did. As Gwynne describes him, "This was the quintessential Quanah: hustling, demanding, always looking for an angle, always negotiating yet unwilling to compromise his own principles."[54]

Reading this description, I couldn't help but think of Manny Jules. Unlike Quanah, though, Jules and his father before him managed to forge a path for the First Nations of British Columbia, if not Canada as a whole. The Comanches couldn't adapt in time, but the Kamloops band may manage to do so, thanks largely to leaders like Jules. He can't force Aboriginal Peoples to adopt private property on their lands, but if things go as he has planned, he'll provide them with the opportunity to do so. Future leaders will be able to thank Jules and his allies for letting them take control of their own economic and political destiny.

"What Quanah had that the rest of his tribe in the later years did not was ... boundless optimism. Quanah never looked back, an astonishing feat of will for someone who had lived in such untrammeled freedom on the open plains, and who had endured such a shattering transformation. In hard times he looked resolutely forward to something better."[55]

For Manny Jules, something better could be right around the corner.

CHAPTER TWO

Money Instead of Freedom

The Loophole Economy and the Politics of Poverty

LUCILLE BROOKS IS PERCHED at an empty conference table in the neat new office of the sprawling Seneca government building in upstate New York. Dressed in a gray pantsuit and pumps and wearing tasteful pendant earrings and a striking Indian necklace, Brooks looks nothing if not professional. Her bookshelves are lined with thick binders of regulations, but there are few papers lying around. Light streams in through the glass door that welcomes people to the Seneca Nation of Indians Economic Development Company. SNIEDC, as it is known, was launched to help members of the Seneca Nation start businesses, by offering them not only loans but also technical assistance to help them create business plans and grow their already existing enterprises. It's officially certified by the U.S. Treasury as a Community Development Financial Institution (CDFI).

And yet I see no clients here. After my initial interview with Brooks, I walked by the office several more times during the day. The only people in the office were Brooks and her assistant. The phone isn't exactly ringing off the hook either. Indeed, this small business incubator hasn't

47

incubated much at all, Brooks acknowledges. There are a couple of small businesses – a logging company, for instance – that have come to SNIEDC for loans to purchase more equipment. The SNIEDC website lists three clients – a bakery, a Subway franchise, and a company that makes radiant heating technology. But the members of the Seneca Nation seem largely uninterested in or unaware of SNIEDC, now in its 20th year of existence.

SNIEDC loans seem like a perfect opportunity for anyone with the slightest inclination to start a small business. Just a few blocks away, the main streets of the town of Salamanca (2010 population: 5,815) are lined with empty storefronts. Upstate New York has experienced a degree of economic depression for more than half a century, but it's nothing compared to what you'll find in Seneca territory. You'd think people would be queued up around the block to take advantage of the opportunities Brooks has to offer. SNIEDC gives out what it calls "micro-loans" of up to $250,000, with no collateral necessary. Indeed, until recently, no one even did a credit check on the applicants. You won't get a better deal from your own parents.

Truth be told, though, there's not a lot of entrepreneurial spirit on the Allegany and neighboring Cattaraugus territories. As Brooks explains, "The sense is that the annuities have created an entitlement attitude, and that is the downfall. The annuities have enabled people not to work." The annuities that Brooks mentions are drawn from casino revenues.

In 2002, desperate to change its financial situation, the Seneca Nation entered into a gaming compact with New York State, which granted the nation the exclusive right to build and operate three gaming facilities. The decision wasn't an easy one for the tribe. Some people worried that casinos would destroy the culture and traditional religion of the Seneca people. Others worried about its moral impact or worried that Seneca leaders would use casinos to increase their influence in ways that would leave other factions out in the cold. Ultimately, however, in light of the success of other tribal gambling enterprises, there was no other way to go.

The Seneca Niagara Casino opened its doors in 2002, and a luxury hotel followed in 2005. The Seneca Allegany Resort and Casino opened in 2007, and the Seneca Buffalo Creek Casino followed in 2013.

The Seneca Nation has made well over $1 billion in profits off of these facilities. And during the past decade, that largesse has begun to trickle in ever-larger amounts into the hands of the Seneca people. The current annuity for an adult between the ages of 18 and 60 on the reservation is about $8,000, disbursed in quarterly payments. Elders get a larger amount, in a kind of American Indian social security program. Half the money for children under 18 is given to their parents, and the other half is put into a trust. When a Seneca youth turns 18 and can show he or she has graduated from high school or earned a GED, he or she receives a lump sum of $30,000. Those who don't get a high-school degree have to wait until they're 21 to receive the money. With each passing year, the annuities get larger, because the tribe invests its earnings.

Government officials and other members of the nation tell me that the best thing most young adults do with this money is buy a new truck. These are kids who have never had very much before; someone hands them a huge check and they clearly don't know what to do. Store owners report that young people will come in to buy candy and hand over $50 or $100 without expecting any change. These young people seem to have no concept of saving or investing. They're not unlike lottery winners, who tend to be no better off a few years after hitting the jackpot than they were before. According to the National Endowment for Financial Education, about 70 percent of those incurring a financial windfall lose that money within a few years. There's apparently something about *earning* money that makes people less willing to spend it unwisely.

Instead of giving Indians more control over their own land – allowing them to develop natural resources in ways that respect their own views of the environment or to use land as collateral to start their own

businesses – we've offered them what you might call a loophole economy. We allow Indians to engage in enterprises that we can't or won't
have in other neighborhoods.

It used to be selling tax-free cigarettes, liquor, and gasoline. Then it
was the gaming industry. Now, more states are allowing casinos to be
run by non-Indians, and casinos aren't the source of profit they once
were. But never fear. The Justice Department decided in December
2014 to allow marijuana to be grown on reservations – even if the drug
is illegal in the state where the reservation is located.

Gambling, cigarettes, alcohol, drugs – who wouldn't want these
businesses to form the economic backbone of their community? In
some cases, these businesses have proved very profitable for tribes. For
most, though, these are hardly viable paths to economic growth. And
they bring all sorts of problems with them.

Deron Marquez, who served as chairman of the San Manuel band
of Mission Indians in Southern California from 1999 to 2006, says that
the upside of his tribe's bingo parlor is obvious. The tribe has more
money to spend on health care, education, and housing. But the gaming business – particularly the payments that members of the tribe
receive from it – has created problems, too. "For anyone in society
who has addictive behavior, we are making addiction stronger with
per capita payments. We've become the enabler." But even for people
who don't have problems already, Marquez says it's "hollow money. It's
just a new kind of government program – a tribal government program."

The results are just like the results of government dependency anywhere. As Marquez notes, "The apathy becomes overwhelming. The
payments can create an atmosphere [where] why would you have to
do anything?"

To try to address this problem, the Seneca tribe recently ran a financial
literacy program for high-school students, which sounded pretty elementary. The organizers gave the teens pretend checks and had them
go to a "bank" to cash the checks or deposit them. Then they could

spend the money on a variety of goods and services. Stephen Scott, who's helping Senecas complete an application to open a credit union on the territory, explains to me that few of the kids saved or invested any of their money. And they seemed unwilling or unable to distinguish "wants from needs." He shows me one of the play hundred-dollar bills from the exercise. On one side, it says "First Nations Development Institute." On the other, it says "The Native Nations of America: In the Creator We Trust."

For all they understand of its value and its potential to change their lives, the real money they receive on their 18th birthday might as well be Monopoly money.

But Scott, who has worked with other tribes that have benefited from casino revenues, says that Senecas actually have things more under control than most. When he worked for the Shakopee Mdewakanton tribe in Minnesota, they were giving out $80,000 to kids who had just turned 18. As a result of the handouts, he says, "There was no drive to work. No drive to further their education. It caused drugs and alcohol to be rampant. There was a lot of stress on families, the breakdown of families, addiction to gambling."

Indeed, wasting the money is a largely harmless consequence of this windfall – compared to the alternative. For example, many young Senecas use the money to purchase drugs or alcohol. There's a serious drug problem on the two territories. Every couple of miles, a pair of sneakers hangs on a telephone line, a sign that a drug dealer is open for business nearby. And government officials tell me that the dealers know when quarterly checks are sent out, so they're particularly visible then. According to Scott, there's also violence toward older members of the nation, who get larger checks. "Elders are being abused by their grandsons to support whatever habit they have. We have a lot of break-ins."

The tribe has been debating various methods of either putting off the big check until these kids are older and more responsible or putting constraints on the ways the money can be used.

I meet two young women having lunch together in the vast common area of the tribal government building. While they pick at their take-out, we talk about how they came to be among the few in their cohort who went to college and stayed on the straight and narrow path to a career. They both graduated from high school just as the lump-sum payments were beginning, when the payments weren't very large. One used her money to pay for some expenses while she was taking classes at the local community college. She tells me, "Some kids get a car, alcohol, or drugs." She says that the local high schools should offer seniors classes on how to invest the money.

Her friend says that a lot of people blow the money on a vacation or even gambling. And it's with a particular show of disdain that she talks about the ones who go into the casino or the bingo hall. "Gambling is a disease," she tells me. "We go to the casino to eat and to watch people. They just stare at those machines," she says, referring to the thousands of slot machines that line the floors of the casinos. "People lose their homes there."

Of course, most of the people who go to the Seneca Allegany Casino and Resort are not Seneca themselves. They've traveled from all over the country to this enormous glass structure built into the side of a hill on the side of the interstate. The multilevel parking structure has spaces reserved for the most loyal customers.

It has become almost cliché to observe that casinos are depressing places. But they really are. In the Allegany Casino, there are pictures of nature everywhere – wild horses, sunsets over mountains – but almost no windows to speak of. Even the nonsmoking rooms reek of cigarettes. There's no natural light inside, so customers don't realize how much time has gone by while they're throwing away their money. Indeed, it's hard to find a clock anywhere in the cavernous facility. There are a few tables for card playing, but as the young ladies I ran into observed, mostly there are rows and rows of slot machines, each with different themes – beaches, fruit, cars.

By 8:00 A.M., a smattering of tourists have already planted themselves in front of these flashing screens. The crowd is mostly working-class. A lot of the customers are overweight and regularly call the waitresses over to order more soda. A disproportionate number of people are in wheelchairs.

The restaurants in the casino – there are at least three – feel like the ones in Disney World. They're overpriced – think Manhattan steak house – but people pay to eat there because they don't want to stop gambling, and, truth be told, you'd have to drive a ways to get a decent meal outside of the casino anyway.

But there aren't as many customers as there were just a few years ago. And there are likely to be fewer in the future, because New York State recently granted licenses to three more large non-Indian gambling facilities, two in the same upstate area where the Senecas operate.

Although Governor Andrew Cuomo touts the expansion of casinos as a plan for economic growth upstate, most observers see a downward trend. The Mashantucket Pequot tribe, which runs the Foxwoods Resort in Connecticut, once paid its thousand or so members more than $100,000 annually from its profits, but in 2012 they got nothing. Some moved elsewhere in search of work. The casino was $1.7 billion in debt and was closing its nearby Pequot Museum for several months. Tribe officials wouldn't explain exactly why, but according to the *New York Times*, most of the staff were laid off.[1] Since then the museum has continued to close annually during the slower winter months.

Part of the problem is competition. Gambling can only expand so far, warns E. J. McMahon at the Empire Center for Public Policy in Albany: "There is a finite market for this. There's only so much revenue to go around."

After that, you're stuck playing politics to keep what you have. In his contribution to the volume *Self-Determination: The Other Path for Native Americans*, economist Ronald Johnson notes, "Now that it has been demonstrated how successful Indian gaming operations can be, there is no reason to suspect that gaming tribes will be spared the political pressures that beset the commercial gaming industry or any other successful industry dependent on governmental support or acquiescence."[2]

Indeed, tribes have spent millions lobbying to ensure that they keep the corner on certain area markets. But they seem to have had limited success. Politicians want to get as much money as they can out of the gaming industry, which means, they seem to think, opening it up to more players. There's an agreed-upon buffer zone, in which non-Indian casinos may not set up shop, around the New York Indian casinos. But the casinos are typically frequented by folks from outside the area, and now that there'll be establishments much closer to New York City, it's unlikely many people will head up to Allegany for their slot-machine needs.

Cuomo says that the new casinos will create more than 3,600 permanent jobs, including 1,300 in Schenectady County, 1,050 in Sullivan County, and 1,250 in Seneca County. "This is more job growth in Schenectady than has probably happened in a century, so it is exciting," Cuomo said.[3]

Well, maybe.

Seneca leaders, for their part, say they've seen the writing on the wall for some time now. They believe they got into the gambling industry just as it was reaching its peak. And although they've been happy to ride the wave, they do want to prepare for the future, which they hope won't look like that of their brethren in Connecticut.

Michael Kimelberg is probably one of the main reasons that Seneca finances will survive the decline of gambling. Kimelberg spent part of his childhood on the territory. His mother was a member of the Seneca Nation, but his father was not. He spent some time in Albany but came back every summer to be with his relatives. His great-great uncle was the president of the tribe in the 1960s. His mother was very active in the nation's leadership as well.

After attending college at SUNY Geneseo, Kimelberg went to the University of Washington for graduate school. He stayed in the Northwest to go into planning and development. By 2010 the nation had made some significant profits from the casino and was starting to think more about development projects.

Indeed, one advantage of the gaming revenues, even if they aren't a panacea, is that they can be used to lure talented people back to Indian territories. The reversal of the brain drain has been more feasible in the Northeast and Northwest than for the plains Indians. Even though Seneca territory is in a depressed area of New York, parts of the territory are less than an hour from Buffalo, and there are other metropolitan areas relatively nearby as well. There are opportunities in the area for spouses of Senecas who want to come back to work for the tribe too. Rural South Dakota this is not.

So Kimelberg returned to be in charge of development and planning and then in 2012 became the chief operating officer of the Seneca Nation. He lives with his wife and family in Buffalo, drives a Mercedes station wagon and spends his days trying to figure out how to sustain and grow the wealth and influence of the Seneca Nation for generations to come. When he looks back on the debate the tribe had over whether to open the casinos, he says, "I think it was wise to be circumspect.... Folks like the Pequots were doing quite well, so there was certainly a lot there, but gaming is by no means a fantasy.... Credit has to be given to our policymakers early on, who recognized that gaming is a volatile industry."

Kimelberg actually returned to New York a year after the nation hired his brother David. David Kimelberg had been working as general counsel for a venture capital group in Boston and was reluctant to return. But he too was persuaded. The tribe had committed $28 million over five years to diversify the tribe's holdings. Seneca Holdings was formed as a limited liability company, with an independent board chosen by the tribal leadership. But how it was going to invest its money was a little less clear.

For the first few months he was back on the territory, David, who became the CEO of Seneca Holdings, wasn't actually sure what he was supposed to be doing. A couple of years earlier, the tribe had applied for a license to operate a radio station. So David spent six months building a state-of-the-art commercial radio station. Which wasn't exactly what he was hired to do. "It wasn't an ask," he tells me. "It was more of a directive." But today the station "breaks even," and he says it has created "a lot of social capital." There's a sense that David also built up the trust of some of the other community members with this project.

As an outsider who came back, David has faced skepticism from other Senecas. And one member of the tribal council asks whether I happen to know David, because I'm Jewish, and, well, you know.

In a meeting with three members of the tribal council, it's easy to see some suspicion still bubbles beneath the surface. Jeffrey Gill, who worked as an artist and then had a career in law enforcement before joining the council, says that he supports David and Michael's efforts. "The only disagreement I have with this administration," he says, "is that the decision should be made by the tribal council ... and not be pushed or placed in front of us that this is the way it's going to be."

David started with a difficult task, though. As he notes, it's hard to match the margins of gaming. "It was a $750-million-a-year business, which delivers incredible margins." And the tribe had a "monopoly advantage" on gaming as well. Other sectors weren't going to deliver those margins, but as David notes, the nation has some advantages in other areas. "We are a sovereign nation within the U.S.... We have some tax efficiencies. We have regulatory advantages. We have all these really cool things that could be leveraged."

Indeed, the Seneca people have a long history of leveraging their sovereign advantages, beginning with selling cigarettes and gasoline tax-free on the reservations. For many years after states imposed sales taxes on those two commodities, businesses on Indian territories attracted customers with their significantly lower prices. Although their economies weren't exactly thriving as a result, many small businesses were able to pull in some pretty startling margins – one Seneca leader suggests that business owners regularly made 300 percent profit on these items.

In 1991, profits began to taper off with the settlement of the case of *Oklahoma Tax Commission v. Citizen Band, Potawatomi Indian Tribe of Oklahoma.* The Supreme Court held that although tribes needn't charge tax to their own members, they did have to collect tax if they sold cigarettes to nonmembers. Enforcement of the law was difficult, for obvious reasons. Are you really going to prove that you're an Indian every time you buy cigarettes? What counts as proof? Why can't you buy them for someone standing outside the store? In principle, it could be no more difficult than checking someone's ID before the purchase of liquor. But in some areas, enforcement was simply nonexistent, because the reporting procedures for taxation required by the federal government and by the individual states weren't the same as the ones on the territories.

The real change came in 2010 with the passage of the Prevent All Cigarette Trafficking Act (the PACT Act), whose goal was to halt the sale of untaxed cigarettes online. The main idea was to limit the sales of cigarettes to minors – who knows how many kids were going online to order their smokes? – and to limit the black market in cigarette sales, which the feds said was being used to fund organized crime and even terrorist activities. The major effect of the new law, though, was to ensure that online and mail-order retailers couldn't evade state and federal taxes.

The result, explains Michael A. John, the manager of the Small Business Incubator Program on the territory, was "major economic devastation" on the territory. The businesses that weren't meeting the reporting requirements had to close down. For others, without the advantage of being able to offer cigarettes tax-free, their profit margins plunged. John says that the problem was that these businesses simply couldn't undercut the competition off the reservation anymore.

Which brought the tribe to their second sovereign advantage: gambling. Although many tribes had traditions of playing games of chance, such as dice, there was little effort to turn these into moneymaking enterprises until the 1970s. In that decade, several tribes, including the Seneca, opened up bingo parlors and other small-scale gambling operations. The state governments, though, wanted to have jurisdiction over these businesses. They argued that not only should they be able to limit the number of casinos and bingo parlors, they should get a share of the revenue.

The 1998 Indian Gaming Regulation Act (IGRA) largely cemented the notion that in this regard, Indian lands were sovereign and answerable only to the federal government, not to the state governments. So, for instance, it's the FBI that has jurisdiction over Indian casinos, not local or state police.

But as states started to allow and expand gaming operations off the reservation, that sovereign advantage began to evaporate. Which left David Kimelberg looking for the next big thing, the third sovereign advantage.

"What we did," he tells me, "is we went all in on government contracting." As David notes, "we have some very interesting contracting preferences by virtue of being the Seneca."

Seneca Holdings is now a sort of umbrella company for several contracting firms. The company can be taken to court by other parties in case there is a dispute. Seneca Holdings has its own board. As David says, "If things go sideways, then [other parties] have full recourse." But the suit can't go any higher up the chain. In other words, the nation's other assets can't be taken in any legal action. Not only does this protect the Seneca tribe, it gives its business partners assurance that the tribe won't try to use its sovereign status to evade the federal or state laws by which their contracts are governed.

Seneca Holdings has formed four operating companies – one for construction, one for telecommunications, one for IT, and one for security. Anywhere from 50 to 80 percent of their work is for the federal government, including the Department of Defense, the Army Corps of Engineers, and the Bureau of Indian Affairs. Seneca Holdings companies have built an anti-terrorist center in Schenectady. They handle the telecom and IT needs of an army base in Florida. And David hopes they'll soon be closing on a contract to put up antennae for an army base in South Korea. They operate in 33 states as well as overseas.

The Seneca companies have what the Small Business Administration refers to as 8(a) certification, which means they're eligible for preferential treatment from the federal government because they're owned and controlled by members of an economically disadvantaged group. Even when they're bidding for private contracts, though (with firms like Wal-Mart), they often have an advantage, since there are major companies that – for public relations purposes, if not legal ones – give preference to female- and minority-owned businesses.

Still, David insists that the Senecas couldn't have been as successful as they have with these companies if they weren't doing good work. Other nations, he says, have made the mistake of assuming that business would just fall into their laps once they were 8(a) certified. "It's not a be-all [and] end-all," David says. "It's a great entrée," but the Seneca companies have had to actively seek both the federal and private contracts they want – and do a good job too. Federal work, especially, he says, is "incredibly relationship-driven." If you can show that you do good work, they'll hire you again.

The plan has worked out well, as far as David and the tribal leadership can see. Indeed, this kind of diversification no doubt has the potential to insulate the tribe from the economic and political ups and downs of gaming. But it also is not a panacea.

Congress has been scrutinizing the 8(a) provisions for Native populations. The preferences have been widely used by Alaskan Native Corporations. Senator Claire McCaskill of Missouri wrote a letter to the Small Business Administration in the summer of 2014 questioning the widespread use of this provision. "Many ANCs have grown to the multi-million dollar corporations that are among the largest federal contractors. In 2009, I held a hearing that highlighted my concerns about ANCs' participation in the 8(a) program, including a lack of oversight by SBA, the use of ANCs to circumvent the federal contracting process, and that the benefits were not reaching disadvantaged Alaskan natives."[4] Certainly non-Native companies like Boeing (headquartered in Missouri) have complained that they're losing federal contracts to companies that are hardly disadvantaged (even if the ancestors of the people at their helm were historically subject to discrimination).

Ultimately, David sees these kinds of government preferences shrinking, which is why he's trying to increase the number of jobs that Seneca takes through competitive bidding processes. In the meantime, though, he's also on the lookout for the next sovereign advantage.

David is doubtless a smart investor, and Senecas are lucky to have him and his brother looking out for the tribe's long-term financial future. But their strategy is also creating problems for the tribe itself. Many people here are bitter. Every time one of these "sovereign advantages" disappears, the men and women of the Seneca Nation feel as if the state of New York or the federal government has just screwed them over again.

Justin Schapp, a special assistant to the treasurer for the Seneca Nation, sums up this attitude: "Before any Native nation can deal with any of their community issues in their midst, they have to go under the microscope that is the U.S. federal government or the state telling them that they want to share the pie – often it's the lion's share."

Schapp continues, "They extract from us even today. It's extraction, extraction, extraction. You work, and we own you." He asks me, "You want to get down to the brass tacks of what my personal feelings are? I feel like I am owned. When I say I'm Seneca, then I am owned by either the state or federal government."

And Schapp, who's college-educated and employed at a high level by the nation, probably has a better idea than most people do of the history of the tribe's economic strategies. In some way, he probably understands that the tribe's leaders have tried to find loopholes in federal and state law that they can exploit to gain a financial step up. Perhaps he feels that the least the U.S. government can do after treating Indians so badly for so long is look the other way when Indian leaders use these strategies.

But he and other Senecas I've spoken to see this history through a particular lens, something like this: First the white people took our lands; then they ran our convenience stores out of business; now they've brought in competition to kill our casinos. Pretty soon, we won't have our advantage in federal contracting. What's left?

The problem with the strategy of rent-seeking to achieve economic growth isn't that it won't work in the short term. Indeed, the Seneca people will probably have a hefty pile of cash at their disposal for the foreseeable future. But for individual members of the nation, the tribal government's strategy can prove deeply disheartening. Why start a business when the federal government is just going to swoop in and take away your profits? If there's a reason besides the annuities that's keeping members of the Seneca Nation from visiting Brooks and asking for a loan from SNIEDC, it's probably this: they simply feel beaten by the system.

David Kimelberg argues, though, that strengthening the hand of the tribe was his first priority when he came to this position a few years ago. To explain why, David takes me back to the 1960s, when his great-uncle was president and the Army Corps of Engineers wanted to build a dam to the south of the Allegany territory. The city of Pittsburgh was flooding along the Allegheny River, and so, over Seneca objections, President Kennedy approved construction of the Kinzua Dam in 1961. It was completed in 1965, but in the process, 10,000 acres of the Allegany territory were condemned and more than 700 Senecas were displaced.[5]

David and many of his fellow Senecas are still rightfully angry about what happened. "The nation had no resources, back then," he recalls. "We got some lawyers pro bono and some reassurances from President Kennedy." His uncle even went on national television to discuss it. But ultimately, they were "steamrolled" – "they set people's houses on fire and then flooded the whole area. It was incredibly traumatic."

That, says David, "would not happen today. If someone said they wanted to put our territory under water today, there would be so many lawyers and congressmen here." He's right. The Seneca have amassed enough cash and influence now that it'd be very hard for the government to do anything to their land without their permission. In addition, of course, the environmental and political movements protecting Indian lands have gotten significantly stronger in the intervening decades. Any actions would be tied up in court indefinitely.

Though it's ultimately more important that Senecas "have a good standard of living and mortality rates that are lower than the general population," David says, you won't get those things when you have a federal or state government running roughshod over you.

He compares Seneca territory to the state of Israel. "People want to bomb you out of existence, and you just need to make sure that doesn't happen."

It's an interesting analogy. It's tempting to dismiss the idea that the U.S. government is actively trying to destroy Seneca lands in the same way, say, that Syria is trying to destroy Israel. But the creation of the dam has clearly made a deep impression on Seneca leaders and members. If the territory can be taken away at the stroke of a presidential pen, then surely anything is possible.

Even granting the idea that Senecas have to be worried about their survival, one wonders whether trying to strengthen the hand of the nation from the top down without really improving the lives of individual citizens is the right strategy. After all, Israel has managed to do both. Its citizens somehow manage to lead 21st-century lives, with the latest technology and many other luxuries. They pursue education, earn money, and raise stable families, all while trying to ensure that their country survives. Some might argue that their country's ability to survive is tied inextricably to the strength of its citizens, not just the size of its treasury.

Though Senecas have financial advantages that other American Indians don't, they haven't let go of the idea that their problems can be solved from the top down. So, for instance, in order to encourage members to open small businesses, the nation commissioned a survey of businesses within a certain distance of the territory. This, says Michael A. John, "allows us to show the saturation market for business opportunity." Thanks to this survey, when people come to the tribal leadership saying they want to open up a pizza business, "we can say there happen to be *x* amount of pizza businesses in the area. When you figure out all of your expenses and all of your payments and finances, you're making 3 cents on the dollar, so would it be profitable for you to do a pizza business?" On the other hand, they found that there was potential in the area of "outdoor recreation, maintenance, landscaping, and professional massage."

John and his colleagues are trying to be helpful, but telling citizens when there's room for another pizza business and how much of a profit they'd need to turn to make it worthwhile isn't how thriving economies are developed. What if someone had a cheaper way of making pizza, or what if they made better pizza and customers preferred them to the competition? These questions don't seem to occur to the people running the tribal government. And why would they? Nor is the government very good at figuring out who'd be good at landscaping or whether there's a workable economic model for a professional masseuse nearby.

You don't need to travel to Beijing to see central planning at work. It's everywhere on reservations.

For the Seneca tribe, though – unlike, say, the Sioux or the Northern Cheyenne – the problem isn't finding employment for its members. There are about 8,000 enrolled members. About 2,000 of them work for the tribal government in some capacity, and 3,000 work for the casinos. Even assuming that there'll be fewer casino jobs in the future, it does seem as though the Seneca Nation has insulated itself from economic downturn. It has a lot of money in its coffers, and there are still relatively few enrolled members (though thanks to the high birthrate and the fact that joining the tribe can get you a share of the annuities, enrollment has been growing). Indeed, rather than turning into Israel, Senecas have created in upstate New York a kind of oil-rich sheikhdom like Saudi Arabia.

Although this kind of wealth – which goes directly into the public coffers and is doled out in small amounts to citizens – can provide societies with a safety net, protecting them from the deepest kinds of poverty, it can also hamper development. In a 2001 paper for the journal *World Politics*, UCLA professor Michael Ross argues that oil revenues have actually hampered the development of democracy in Arab states.[6] These governments use low tax rates and patronage jobs to dampen opposition to them. The "no representation without taxation" stance now has significant support among scholars of political science, who observe that although in most cases economic development hastens democratic participation (because governments must be accountable to the people who pay for them), governments whose money comes from natural resources are in a different position.

This is not to say that democracy doesn't exist in Seneca territory, but there are both a lot of patronage jobs to be had and a seemingly great deal of dissatisfaction among the members. Relatively recently, in 1995, there was actually a shootout on the reservation between two rival factions, each claiming the tribal presidency. Three people were killed, and one was wounded. The president at the time had been accused of buying votes and proceeding with negotiations over the casino even after a tribal referendum had rejected it.[7]

As John Mohawk, a teacher in the American studies program at the State University at Buffalo and a reservation resident, told the *New York Times*, "Then there were accusations of wrongdoing again and again, and meetings increasingly closed to the public, and very frustrated people without anything to do because there were no rules with teeth in them. That led to the pushing, the punches, the kicks, the rock-throwing, and eventually led to the gunfire."[8]

Today, things are much calmer. But although people like the Kimelberg brothers have stable long-term jobs, most of the government service positions vary depending on who the president of the nation is. There's not really a significant "civil service." Every two years, the entire administration of the nation switches between two locations – one on the Allegany and one on the Cattaraugus territory. And the president can't serve two consecutive terms.

Whether through the casino or the government, most of the jobs held by folks on the territories are publicly funded. Although the telecom company is helping install a high-speed wireless network throughout the Cattaraugus territory and is doing some work in the Niagara Falls area as well, Seneca Holdings doesn't contribute much to the employment of nation members, because most of the jobs aren't local and because most enrolled members of the Seneca Nation don't have the skills to perform these jobs anyway.

But the Seneca tribe's efforts to exploit its sovereign advantage – and the problems that result from that advantage – beg the most important question: what exactly do we mean when we talk about the sovereign status of Indian nations? The tribal government exists in a kind of netherworld where, for instance, there can be signs on government buildings naming Jesus Christ the Lord because constitutional protections against the establishment of religion don't apply. And the machinations of tribal government, unlike most federal and state governing institutions, often take place behind closed doors, with little transparency. Many newspapers on reservations are funded by the tribal government and, as such, are subject to tribal leaders' whims. Meanwhile reporters at independent newspapers have trouble getting access to government proceedings. In the spring of 2015, the tribal council at Pine Ridge requested that local businesses stop selling the *Rapid City Journal* because tribal leaders disliked an article it ran.[9]

After President Obama visited the Standing Rock Sioux reservation in North Dakota, the *Grand Forks Herald* editorialized that if the president were serious about fixing the problems that plague reservations, guaranteeing freedom of the press would be a good start.[10]

Cases like that of Peter MacDonald in the 1980s, the so-called Navajo Watergate, drew attention to the problem of corruption in tribal governments and to the fact that it was unclear whether a tribal council could oust a leader who accepted millions of dollars in kickbacks. Matters have improved somewhat since then, but the truth is that when it came to helping the tribes set up a governing structure, this country left American Indians somewhere before Enlightenment Europe.

How much power tribal governments have is a matter of continued dispute. The word "sovereignty" is thrown around on reservations like it's going out of style, but no one's quite sure what it means these days.

As you enter reservations across the country, you'll find ominous signs warning that you're subject to the laws of the tribe and the territory. Are you no longer then subject to the laws of the state? Or the federal government? Are you no longer entitled to the protections you enjoy as a citizen of the United States? Maybe these seem like esoteric questions, but such issues are regularly tested in our courts, and no consistent answers have been arrived at.

When I asked Schapp, assistant to the treasurer of the Seneca Nation, about sovereignty, he told me that he dreamed of a time when his nation would be seen the way they are when playing lacrosse at the World Games – that is, as a nation separate from the United States and respected as its own independent national entity in a "globalized world."

Tribal leaders can continue to claim that tribes are nations apart, but no legal authority takes seriously the idea that the relationship between any Indian community and Washington is the same as the one between Washington and Paris, for example. And if tribal authorities *were* serious about it, they'd stop accepting payments from the federal government, for one thing. As far as we know, the United States isn't subsidizing housing in the south of France.

The battle over tribal sovereignty isn't simply a semantic one. The ambiguity of the relationship between tribal leaders and the federal government has created a situation whereby Indians demand more autonomy but instead are offered more money – like candy to appease a crying toddler. Indeed, the trust authority has created a relationship whereby Indians will forever be treated as children, incapable of standing on their own two feet. The time for grandstanding is over. The American government does have a responsibility to Indians, but it's not to send them checks while pretending to engage in international diplomacy.

Is there a different path for American Indians? A way out of the loophole economy and the dependence engendered by the false promise of sovereignty? A trip to North Carolina gives a clue.

Robeson County, North Carolina – which in 1993 briefly gained infamy as the place where basketball legend Michael Jordan's father was murdered in a carjacking – is the poorest in the state. Close to half the children here live below the poverty line. Approximately 44 percent of the households with dependent children are headed by single mothers.[11]

I interviewed one woman outside her trailer home. As her dog barked at me threateningly, she described how she had been caring for the combined five children of both her brother and her sister, who were both in prison (one for failing to appear in court, the other for stealing checks from mailboxes). She herself had lost custody of the children temporarily when her electricity was shut off after she failed to pay the bill for several months. The family was in the news in 2010 when the now-jailed sister left her 3-year-old unattended and the boy drowned in a nearby drainage ditch.[12]

But grinding poverty and dysfunction aren't the only story here. There's significant economic activity in the area, as well as stretches of middle-class homes. Thanks to haphazard zoning laws, you can often see trailer parks between well-kept split ranch homes. And some of the real estate is even nicer – new two-story colonial or restored Victorian.

This doesn't look like a reservation, at least not the kind you'll find in Montana or South Dakota. But it is the home of the Lumbee Indians. Although the Lumbees gained recognition from the federal government in 1956, they weren't given any particular parcel of land on which to live. Nor have they been given many of the protections or financial benefits that come with being of Indian descent.

In part, this odd limbo is the result of confusion about Lumbee ancestry. Historical accounts suggest that the Lumbees lived in the swampy lowlands of North Carolina at least as far back as the early 18th century. Settlers encountered people they described as "light-skinned Indians" and "a mixt Crew, a lawless people," some of whom bore the name Locklear, still among the most common Lumbee surnames today.[13]

If you ask Ben Chavis, a Lumbee, why the Lumbees were never forced off this land as so many of their brethren were – the Cherokee and Navajo used to occupy vast swaths of the American South before they were pushed west – he'll tell you, "The land was so worthless, no one ever bothered."

As Fergus Bordewich says of Lumbee territory, "The swamps were a terra incognita without newspapers or schools; even churches were so rare that births, marriages and deaths went unrecorded."[14] Eventually the swamps were drained and the land was used for farming tobacco and cotton. Lumbees, who had been living a mostly isolated existence, also began to mingle more with whites and free blacks – to the point that today Lumbees do not have any distinct racial characteristics.

Bordewich suggests that this is one of many factors that have made gaining recognition from the federal government and even gaining respect from other tribes difficult. "The Lumbees challenge almost every preconception of what Indians should be. . . . They run the physical gamut from blond hair and blue eyes to the nearly Negroid. They have no chiefs or medicine men and no reservation. They have no memory of the tribe from which their ancestors may have come, nor the language they spoke, nor of any religion older than the pious and passionate Baptist faith that, to a person, they today profess."[15]

Whether any of these things should be considered a requirement for being categorized as an American Indian is debatable, though. More than half of all Indians in America don't live on reservations, and many have no sense of their heritage. The vast majority are Christian. A significant portion don't have any distinctly Indian appearance, speak no Native language, and know nothing about traditional language or culture.

But the reason to investigate the Lumbees is that they're a case study in what a community of American Indians can accomplish without a reservation and without the kind of preferences and money that the federal government has offered hundreds of other Indian communities throughout the country. Cheryl Beasley, a professor of nursing at the University of North Carolina at Pembroke, ticks off the number of professionals among Lumbees – doctors, lawyers, nurses, accountants. There are 60 doctors here among 60,000 people. "You don't find that in other tribes," she tells me emphatically. "The Navajos would like to have those numbers." She says that this success comes from the tribe's independence from the federal government. "Indians had to pay for everything themselves here. They had pride in the people who built it." Beasley says she has friends on the Rosebud reservation in South Dakota and she sees how a culture of dependence has taken over there. "They just say to the federal government: 'Give us our check and tell us what to do.'"

What's now the University of North Carolina at Pembroke started off as a grade school for Indians. In 1887, American Indians actually petitioned the General Assembly of North Carolina to help the community educate its children. They received a paltry $500 grant toward the payment of teachers. But it was enough to get things off the ground. Pembroke became a college in the 1930s and part of UNC in 1972. In part because the school has a strong nursing program, there are a great many trained nurses among Lumbees.

But there are also doctors and lawyers and accountants. Beasley's sister Lucy Lowry is a CPA who teaches at the local community college. Four of the Beasley siblings have PhDs, and the other three have master's degrees. Their grandfather was a schoolteacher. They're third-generation college educated, they tell me proudly.

There's a middle class here in Lumberton and in the neighboring towns. Unlike on reservations, people here can own land outright. Lumberton (2010 population: 21,542) is a popular stop on the I-95 corridor, and, in addition to countless fast-food restaurants and motels, the town boasts a Super Wal-Mart. In other words, there's plenty of poverty, but there's also economic activity and opportunity.

One afternoon, I drive with Chavis around town. We stop at various landmarks. There are small cemeteries, each with a few gravestones. The names are all the same – Lowry, Locklear, Oxendine. Lumbees are really only a few large extended families. The larger gravestones are usually for local bigwigs. On one Oxendine stone just off the road, it says, "He was a quiet Indian leader who gave fiercely of his love, time, counsel and wealth to others." Chavis laughs: "Translation: He never had a job."

Chavis believes that because Lumbees don't live on a reservation, they have a chance to succeed that tribes out west simply don't. And though the tribe's story doesn't follow a simple trajectory, his own story supports his belief.

Like many Lumbees of his generation, Chavis managed to work his way up from poverty, get an education, start a career, and live a middle-class life. He grew up in Robeson County, the oldest of six siblings. His abusive father died when he was six years old. And his mother got by on sharecropping and working as a maid.

In his autobiography, *Crazy Like a Fox*, Chavis says that when he was growing up, the family could eat only if his mother earned enough money. According to Chavis, the family once got a visit from a local official to see whether his mother could qualify for food assistance – this was before the food stamp program. She told Chavis's mother that if she wanted help, she'd have to turn over three of her children to the state. She refused, and the family barely scraped by. One night, recounts Chavis, the family had to split one piece of cornbread as their entire dinner.[16]

But that experience motivated him. He's the only one of his siblings to have finished high school, let alone attend college. He earned a track scholarship to Oklahoma City College and a received a doctorate from the University of Arizona before going on to make a small fortune in California real estate. He tells me he remembers being in high school running down the street where his farm is now and dreaming of being wealthy enough to own a house here. He recently bought his parents a home on the street for $30,000.

"There ain't nothing better than pain and fear," Chavis tells me. "I'm fearful in my life that I will go back and live in total poverty as I did as a child. I've got a retirement account. That don't mean nothing. I'm still afraid."

Whatever it was that brought Chavis to where he is today, he's not alone. Despite the problems that plague this area, Lumbees have managed to avoid some of the worst poverty and dysfunction that affect Indians to the west. Among the men and women I meet who are in their 50s and 60s, there's a strong work ethic, a sense of the importance of education, and a tendency to shake their heads about what has gone wrong in the community over the past few decades.

Sadly, though, the federal government's anti-poverty programs, and now the tribe's likely recognition by the federal government, may mean they're headed down the same path as other Indians.

One afternoon, Chavis and I drive by the local welfare office. The Robeson County Department of Social Services is the largest building for miles – surpassed only by the Super Wal-Mart, I'd guess. There are well over 200 cars in the parking lot, and a woman we encounter from Child Protective Services says at least 300 people work there. The annual budget is about $400 million.

From there, I go to see Dobbs Oxendine at the Toyota dealership he owns. When we pull up, Oxendine is riding around the lot in a golf cart. We retreat to the dealership office, which looks out onto the showroom, and talk about history.

"There has been a real decline," says Oxendine, about his community and his business. He himself finances most of the loans for the cars he sells, because the local banks – even the Indian-owned one – won't give most of his customers a car loan nowadays.

Although he's quick to note that there aren't a lot of opportunities for young people here, he does say that there would be more if the schools were better. "What makes a strong business is education." He recently put out a notice that he was looking for cashiers at the convenience stores he also owns. Some of the applicants hadn't finished high school. The bigger problem, though, says Oxendine, was that "half of the applicants acknowledged that they had been caught shoplifting."

And those are only the ones who admitted it, he adds.

But many of the young men and women in Lumberton simply don't want to work. "They think they can stay at home and make more money in government checks," Oxendine opines. Even the ones he does hire always ask to be paid under the table, so that it doesn't affect their welfare checks.

Oxendine emphasizes, "I don't believe in welfare. You need to give people a pole to fish with." Between food stamps and housing assistance, Oxendine believes that no one has an incentive to work anymore. He describes how things were different when he was growing up: "We had hog killings. We'd give everyone a piece of meat. The church was more involved. We were a very proud people. The giveaways have made us lazy." Oxendine's words hint at the tribe's long tradition of taking care of its members. But he doesn't mistake Lumbees' communal obligations to one another with an obligation for the state or federal government to care for them.

Rosie Hammonds, a woman in her 30s who runs a hair salon in Lumberton, seems to agree with Oxendine's assessment of how things have gone downhill. Hammonds says she has trouble finding people to hire at the salon. Not only are they not hardworking, she says, they don't want other people to succeed. Most of her customers come from nearby Pembroke and other towns, she says, not Lumberton itself, because people in Lumberton are jealous of her success.

The younger generation makes Oxendine shake his head. "They live in public housing. They are children having children. They live from day to day, with no view of tomorrow. They become entitled. They just want to know, 'Where's my check?'"

His daughter Melissa, who works for him, sits in on our conversation. "Churches used to be the welfare office," she explains. "They used to help the elderly and veterans." But now, she laments, it's all the government.

Like the other boomer-generation Lumbees I meet, Oxendine tells me the schools were better when he was growing up. He attended segregated schools – "three schools, three school buses." Like schools for African Americans at the time, Indian schools got used books. "We didn't have lunch rooms or gyms, and there were no jobs for our parents except sharecropping and bootlegging," Oxendine divulges.

But Oxendine nevertheless went on to Pembroke for college. It was mostly a teachers' college at that point, but he says, "Pembroke is the real difference between the Lumbees and other tribes." The fact that they had an institution of higher education that existed long before the tribal colleges came about and the fact that it was incorporated into the University of North Carolina rather than continuing to exist independently ensured that its standards remained high.

His uncle, Hilton Oxendine, opened one of the first restaurants in the area that would serve Indians. He had difficulty securing loans from local banks, but he managed to open the Toyota dealership as well. When he fell on hard times and had to sell the business, Dobbs bought it from him. By the time Dobbs purchased the business, the Lumbee Guaranty Bank had been incorporated.

But Dobbs tells me that he decided instead to go to a "white bank" and find a cosigner for his loan. Because, he explains, "The Lumbee bank's interest rate is always higher."

Dobbs Oxendine used to serve on the tribal council. He chaired a committee that demanded greater recognition for the tribe from the federal government. In 2013, both the House and the Senate introduced bills to offer the Lumbees the same recognition that other tribes have.

The proposed legislation read in part:

The Lumbee Tribe of North Carolina and its members shall be eligible for all services and benefits provided to Indians because of their

73

status as members of a federally recognized tribe. For the purposes of the delivery of such services, those members of the Tribe residing in Robeson, Cumberland, Hoke, and Scotland counties in North Carolina shall be deemed to be residing on or near an Indian reservation.[17]

Although the privileges granted to Lumbees under this act would not extend to gaming – this has been a big sticking point for local officials, and Lumbees have insisted that their application for greater recognition has nothing to do with a desire to open a casino – Lumbees would be eligible for more federal grants to subsidize housing, food, et cetera. And the land itself could be taken into trust by the federal government.

Kay Hagan (D-NC), who introduced the legislation in the Senate, told her colleagues: "Beyond simple fairness, the issue of Lumbee recognition is critically important to the North Carolina economy, and to counties and communities that have been hardest hit by the recent economic downturn."[18]

Hagan argues that Lumbees are in a particularly bad position. As she said, "The Harvard School of Public Health has found that residents of Robeson County have a lower average life expectancy due to persistent poverty and limited access to affordable health care." The proposed legislation, she claimed, would "enable the Lumbee to combat these trends through access to critical programs within Indian Health Services and economic development programs through the Bureau of Indian Affairs."[19]

Just to be clear, Lumbees are already eligible for every form of public assistance that other low-income U.S. citizens may receive, from food stamps to housing assistance to help with energy costs to college financial aid. There are people who argue that these subsidies aren't enough for anyone, but there doesn't seem to be any evidence that Indians in Robeson County are worse off than, say, blacks in Robeson County, and there are plenty of whites and Hispanics living far below the poverty line too.

But Hagan and her colleagues – both Democrat and Republican –

believe that it's the fact that Lumbees are Indians that has led to this poverty, and thus the solutions we've employed to help other Indians are called for in this instance as well. Given the abject failure of the reservation system to allow for, let alone encourage, economic growth in Indian communities, it's nothing less than shocking to hear that politicians in Washington actually want to expand the system.

Oxendine says he has seen where this is all going. But only recently. A few years ago, he says, "I had a change of heart." He started to wonder whether federal recognition would really improve things for his community. "I used to be a professional Indian," he says. "A preacher preaches what his congregation wants to hear." And what the people who elected him wanted to hear was that greater recognition and more money from the federal government could solve their problems.

This is exactly why Chavis has been unimpressed with the Lumbee leadership. He has seen a lot of wheeling and dealing – political influence in exchange for more money to the community – but that, he says, is not the way forward. Lumbees don't need more political influence in North Carolina or in Washington, says Chavis. They need freedom from government, not more government involvement in their lives.

Oxendine has come around to Chavis's point of view. "If we get more checks, we will have more alcohol. It will be detrimental to the Lumbees." As for the idea of having the federal government hold more land "in trust" for his people, he's convinced it's a terrible idea. He has visited many of the reservations out west, and he can only shake his head. "The people out there don't take care of their property." Because it's not their own.

Oxendine is deeply worried about Lumbees' future and the future of the United States, for that matter. "This country is messed up. I'm all right, but my great-grandkids won't be." He tells me, "We need less government in our lives. We used to be a strong country. We need another Ronald Reagan."

If it seems as if Oxendine is some kind of anomaly, he's not. I encounter this attitude frequently among members of his generation. Ronald Hammonds, Rosie's uncle, is a cattle farmer, though he has started to raise buffalo recently because there's a "niche market" for it. He grew up on a farm and thought that he would want to get off of it as soon as possible. Hammond's six children all have college degrees from places like Notre Dame and Chapel Hill. One's a lawyer. One's in the Coast Guard. Another is a CPA. Hammond credits his wife, an educator, with their success. But he says a lot of children their age never learned the value of hard work and education.

"Women are encouraged to have babies. It's economic development. You get a check. We've got more illegitimate kids than ever, and it's getting worse." He calls the local housing project a "breeding ground" and says that the children are mostly being raised by their grandmothers. "They've got no responsibility. They're looking for the government as the solution to all our problems."

So what's his solution? "Cut out the handouts." He believes that the children being raised by their grandparents can go on for "about two more generations and then that horse will be dead." Comparing people to cattle, something people here do with startling frequency, Hammonds tells me, "You've got a kid 25, 35 years old, and they've never been weaned. They don't have a job. . . . You take those calves out there, those calves will suck on that cow, their mama, till they're 600 or 700 pounds. Even when she has another calf, they will continue to suck that cow and the baby won't get any. We're going to have to wean those calves. They ain't going to wean themselves."

He believes that pursuing tribal recognition is a waste of time. "Our problems ain't going to be solved by money. All you're doing is making it worse. It's time for people to take responsibility for their lives, but our government doesn't want them to. They want to be the answer to our problems."

Like many other Lumbees, Hammonds is very happy to not have to deal with the reservation system out west. "The only solution I see," he tells me of the poverty on reservations, is this: "Divide everything up and give it to the Native American family and let them disburse it, spend it, keep it, whatever. I don't need no government taking care of me."

76

With a few exceptions – for example, Social Security and Medic-aid – he believes the federal government should have less involvement in the lives of Native Americans and everyone else for that matter. "They don't need to tell us how to eat . . . who can get married and who can't. That's why the Pilgrims left Europe. We're just getting too regulated." Hammonds says the government "owns too much land to start with. They have no business owning all this land that they took from the Indians."

PART TWO

"White people call it nepotism.

We call it kinship."

CHAPTER THREE

Unprepared

A Narrative of Victimhood

You can drive for miles on the Pine Ridge reservation without seeing another human being. GPS doesn't recognize many of the addresses here in rural South Dakota. Of course, it's possible to drive long distances in the American West without coming upon a major town, but gas stations and convenience stores and fast-food restaurants usually pop up fairly often on the major roads. On Pine Ridge, though, if you don't fill up your gas tank at the right time, you might find yourself out of luck.

To say that this area is rural doesn't really begin to describe it. "Desolate" comes closer. On the first morning of my visit to Pine Ridge, I left my motel and drove toward a school I planned to visit. I traveled almost 40 miles before I saw a place to buy a cup of coffee. I'm told that there used to be a coffee stand at a shack in the motel parking lot, but the owners didn't get enough customers. A couple of locals told me that they couldn't get permission from the Bureau of Indian Affairs to put up a sign on the road.

About 3,000 people live in the Wounded Knee School District in

Manderson, South Dakota. Manderson is in the middle of the Pine Ridge reservation, which makes up most of Oglala Lakota County (formerly Shannon County), the second poorest county in the United States. In 2013, the five police officers assigned to patrol the area received a staggering 16,500 calls for emergency assistance. Sitting at breakfast with me in Rapid City, 100 miles away, Stacy Phelps pauses to let me do the math. Phelps, CEO of the American Indian Institute for Innovation – which has been brought in to "turn around" the Wounded Knee school, among others – wants me to understand the statistics that he's up against.

More than one of the men I interview ask me whether my husband wasn't concerned about me traveling through the reservation alone, particularly at night. A sign in my motel room requests that I use the rag provided rather than bath towels to clean my gun. Statistics are hard to come by, but as of 2009, there were 39 gangs on the reservation, involving more than 5,000 young men. The average life expectancy for men on the reservation is 48, and for women it's 52. Suicide and poor health are partly to blame for those numbers, but so is violence.[1]

With unemployment at more than 80 percent[2] and alcoholism rampant, Pine Ridge is a hard place to grow up. The schools' first job, it has to be said, is to keep children safe. Since Phelps's team took over two years ago, there's general agreement that the school is a calmer place. When I walk through the halls of Wounded Knee – which goes from kindergarten through eighth grade – they're quiet. Although the area outside of the school is run-down, with trailer homes falling apart and trash strewn about, the inside of the school is clean, freshly painted, and bright. It also seems fairly empty – the school operates at less than half of capacity.

Alice Phelps, the newly installed principal and Stacy's sister-in-law, takes me to visit some of the classrooms, where teachers seem to be doing everything in their power to keep things under control. In a second-grade class, the teacher speaks to students in a soothing voice, telling them to "let go of the negative." She asks them to "think about what we can do today to be successful – to make it into third grade." Most of the dozen students seem to be listening while she offers instructions on how to write a friendly (as opposed to formal) letter. After going through the different choices for salutations, she tells them "We don't write mean things in a friendly letter."

While Phelps and I watch the youngest children play in a kindergarten classroom, we talk about their home life. "One weekend a month, we have lock-in," she explains.

"Lock-in?" I ask, wondering what these innocent-looking kids have done to deserve this punishment.

Lock-in is not punishment, she assures me. It's when children stay at school all weekend for safety. Although the weekend is billed as a cultural enrichment event for the children – they sing songs and play traditional games in the school's gym – Phelps tells me that it's timed to coincide with when government checks go out. These are the times when parents are most likely to drink and become abusive, she offers matter-of-factly. Indeed, Wounded Knee's families have earned such a bad reputation that other schools are afraid to send their kids here for basketball games and other community events, Phelps says, because "our parents are so violent and our kids are so disrespectful."

The rhythm of life at Wounded Knee is actually surprisingly dependent on the timing of government subsidies. In the days leading up to food stamp distributions, Phelps finds that kids are particularly hungry and distracted, because there's not enough food at home. The school generally gives kids breakfast, lunch, and snacks, but when they come in on Mondays after a weekend at home, more than one teacher reports that the boys and girls are famished. Right after the food stamps come, many children are absent from school because they're traveling with their families to the other side of the reservation to do grocery shopping.

There are occasional violent incidents at the school. But Wounded Knee has had to learn to deal with them independently. Phelps will occasionally call the police, but she explains that there's usually something more urgent that the police officers have to attend to elsewhere.

Nor does the school get much support from tribal child services. Children who are a danger to themselves or others might be removed briefly, but there aren't many alternative places to keep them. And so the school has to create its own support system as much as possible.

Wounded Knee received a $630,000 school turnaround grant from the federal government in 2014. With the funds, Phelps purchased 40 new computers and was able to finally get curricula and textbooks for reading and math. Before that, the teachers just photocopied from whatever textbook they came across in the school office. Wounded Knee has also instituted a system of "good behavior" incentives, whereby students who participate in class, complete homework assignments, and have no behavior problems can earn time playing on an Xbox or go online in the school's resource room.

Wounded Knee uses a system of incentives for the parents too – which is not uncommon at schools on reservations. At parent-teacher conferences, the school offers door prizes. They conduct drives and give away food – including turkeys on Thanksgiving. The school provides bus service to help parents come to the conferences.

Phelps shows me one innovation of which she's especially proud. Wounded Knee is in the process of installing laundry facilities in one of its buildings for parents to use. The closest Laundromat is more than 50 miles away, and most of the families can't afford washing machines in their own homes. She estimates that the free laundry could save families more than a thousand dollars a year and could be used to lure mothers and fathers for parenting classes and other community activities.

Phelps says her efforts seem to be working – 70 percent of the parents showed up for open house at the beginning of the year, compared with about 30 percent the previous year. The parents themselves are also trying to become more involved in the school and the community. Over the summer, the school asked for help and donations to improve the housing for teachers in Manderson. The donation drives brought in vanities, doors, door handles, cupboard handles, drywall, and paint.

The truth of the matter is that even with improved safety, many parents who live in the district still don't want to send their kids to Wounded Knee. They'd rather have their kids travel hours each day to get something moderately better at a Catholic school or at a public school off the reservation. In a survey, parents reported that the two biggest problems with the school were "bullying" and "low expectations."

Phelps is trying to raise those expectations. "We really want to push them to where they need to be," she tells me. "It has just been a cycle – years of poor teaching – teachers who weren't really driven by data. Everything we do is driven by data."

Phelps is right. The data are deeply depressing. Here's a summary of the situation from a 2013 article in *Education Week*:

> In South Dakota, which has the highest proportion of Native American students of any state, they lag on every academic indicator. According to the state's 2012–13 report card, 42 percent of American Indian students scored "proficient" or "advanced" on state math exams, while 80 percent of white students did so. In reading, 47 percent of American Indian students scored proficient or higher, compared to 79 percent of white students. The four-year graduation rate for South Dakota's American Indian students in 2013 – 49 percent – paints an even grimmer picture. And while the high-school-completion rate, which includes getting a diploma in more than four years or a GED, was much better, at 64 percent, American Indians still trailed every other major subgroup in the state by 17 or more percentage points. In 2009–10, the four-year graduation rate at Pine Ridge High School, the biggest high school on the reservation, was 45 percent.[3]

Phelps's turnaround team aims to bring students up by at least two grade levels this year. "We have seventh-graders who are performing at a third-grade level," Phelps laments.

Despite the improvements that Alice and Stacy Phelps have managed to implement with regard to school safety, my visit to the school left me skeptical of their ability to improve the school's academic record significantly.

At a third-grade class I visited with Alice, students mostly sat at their desks doing math problems, but several had lined up for help from the teacher. Phelps took one boy aside and offered to help him herself.

The first word problem he was struggling with asked, "If a number rounded to the nearest hundred is 400, what is the highest number it could be?" When the student guessed 500, Phelps told him he was correct. The next problem asked, "If a store sold 128 items the first week and 37 more than that the second week, how many did they sell all together?" Phelps instructed the boy to add 128 and 37 to get the answer.

Such misguided help – giving a child the wrong answers to what are probably first-grade math problems – seems nothing short of educational malpractice. It certainly does not inspire confidence.

In other regards, Phelps seems like a very competent woman. When she walks the halls of Wounded Knee, she comes off like someone who means business. Because she reports to the American Indian Institute for Innovation rather than the school board, she has escaped some of the political machinations that plague other schools on the reservation. As she notes, "A lot of times, the schools are the only employment places in the communities. So a lot of times, the family members [of the school board or the tribal leaders] are employed and it's hard to get in there and put in an improvement plan or reprimand someone, let alone put someone out of a job."

I hear this numerous times from other educators. Parents who have relatives on the tribal council or the school board will call teachers or principals to ensure that their kids never receive a failing grade or get held back, even when it's clearly necessary for their child's sake.

Improving the economic situation on reservations isn't just about improving access to capital for residents. It's also, as Winfield Russell, of the Northern Cheyenne tribal council, notes, a human resources problem. Most of the talented young people leave, and those who stay tend to take jobs in the tribal government, putting their talents toward applying for grants from the federal government.

When I ask Crow legislator Conrad Stewart whether he thinks young people on the reservation have the education and the job skills necessary to succeed in today's economy, he becomes very animated. When he was growing up, he says, you didn't see many Crow people working off the reservation – because of discrimination, he suggests. But now, he says, "a lot of times, they don't look at the color of your skin." The result? "Now you've got Crows working at the swimming pool.... You've got Crows working at McDonald's.... You've got Crows working at the truck stop there, a whole mess of Crows working there in Pizza Hut. And you've got Crows working at Papa John's." Finally he mentions: "We've got attorneys."

But what seems clear from this exchange is the fact that tribal leaders are happy even if the only jobs tribe members can get are at the bottom of the economic ladder. And despite my prompting, Stewart sees no problems with the kinds of educational preparation that kids on the reservation are receiving.

Other leaders, like Karl Little Owl, acknowledge that there's a problem with public education on the reservation, but they attribute it to a lack of funding. And Little Owl worries that students are being "bombarded" with too much "standardized testing." There's little evidence, however, that either of these problems explains what's wrong with the schools. In fact, it's striking how officials on Indian reservations offer the same excuses as officials in inner cities to explain the poor performance of local public schools.

As of 2010, only 14.4 percent of students were at or above proficiency levels at Lodge Grass High School, located on the Crow reservation. At Lame Deer, meanwhile, that number was 17.8 percent. And the graduation rates were abysmal too, with only 52 percent from Lodge Grass and 39 percent from Lame Deer graduating on time.[4] According to the Montana Office of Public Instruction, per-pupil spending at Lame Deer was $23,386 for the 2013–14 school year, compared with a statewide average of $10,625.[5] At Lodge Grass it was over $27,304. Reservation schools are among the worst in the nation. They'd give any inner-city school a run for its money when it comes to academic inadequacy and even students' safety.

For many Indian students, their first step out of high school is attending a tribal college. There are now 32 of these schools, which were launched in the 1970s to offer a kind of transition between a reservation high school and a traditional four-year college.

Sadly, tribal college has been an end, not a means. Even Richard Littlebear, the president of Chief Dull Knife College in southeastern Montana, tells me that students are simply getting multiple associate's degrees, not transferring to other schools. There's not much difference, says Littlebear, between Chief Dull Knife and a typical community college. Perhaps that's true, but few of the students seem to be gaining marketable skills – even if there were an actual job market to enter. In addition to courses in IT and mathematics, students can take courses in Native American Studies, Cheyenne Studies, and Arts and Crafts. But the school receives accreditation just like any other community college. And if the students do transfer out – say, to a state university in Montana – they receive two years' worth of credits regardless of what courses they took. But whether they're prepared for the work at a traditional public or private school is another story.

As a 2014 article in the *Atlantic* pointed out, "Despite getting more than $100 million a year in federal funding – including grants low-income students use to pay tuition – tribal colleges often have abysmal success rates."[6] According to a Hechinger Report, the percentage of students who earn a two-year degree within three years or a four-year degree in six years is only 20 percent.[7]

Tribal colleges often compare themselves to historically black colleges and universities (HBCUs), which they say get more money per pupil than tribal colleges. For example, whereas tribal colleges receive a maximum of $8,000 per student, Howard University students get an average of $20,000 per year. But an important question is how much money these colleges are spending per degree awarded. "The Tribal Institute of American Indian Arts in new Mexico," according to the *Atlantic*, "spends $504,000 for every degree it confers ... more than Harvard or MIT."

In fact, the comparison with black colleges is instructive for other reasons. Although the historical impetus for black colleges is clear, the need for them today is less obvious. Black students attending predominantly white institutions have higher graduation rates than those at HBCUs. Since there's no admissions discrimination at other schools – indeed, many colleges would be happy to claim a higher percentage of minority students – perhaps the need for these tribal colleges, just like the need for black colleges, is becoming less urgent. And for those who are truly concerned about young Indian students' economic future, encouraging them to attend higher education institutions off the reservation is probably a better option.

How did things go awry at these tribal colleges? The story of their failures parallels that of many other colleges and universities tasked with helping underprivileged students. First of all, they instituted an open-enrollment policy, which may seem like a good idea, but to anyone who watched the decline of schools like City College in New York as a result of open enrollment, it's clear that a college must have some basic criteria for determining who's qualified to enter. Most students spend at least a year of their time at tribal colleges taking remedial courses.

Of course, because of the dreadful employment situation on the reservations, many students don't have much incentive to get through school. Even if they gain skills in a field like nursing or elementary education, job opportunities are extraordinarily limited. And, truth be told, those jobs are filled just as often by relatives of people in tribal leadership as they are by people who might be more qualified. There's nothing resembling a meritocracy on many of the reservations, and the schools are both a cause and an effect of this problem.

It's also true that these tribal colleges had another mission besides educating kids for careers, which was to help pass on the tribe's culture and language. An admirable goal, no doubt, but one wonders whether that didn't become the primary function of these schools.

Sitting around a table of professors and administrators at Chief Dull Knife one afternoon, it was easy for me to see their compassion, their love of tradition, and their dedication to the students. Once a week, they eat a traditional meal together and speak only the Cheyenne language – they kindly translated for me as they went. They recalled childhoods of simultaneous deprivation and happiness, of large extended families banding together for strength and warmth – for example, when snowstorms left them cut off from neighbors for days, with horses as the only means of transportation.

These elders had high hopes that tribal colleges would provide young people with the best of that extended family life while also preparing them for jobs in the 21st century. As Littlebear explains, the tribal colleges were intended to make students more comfortable, "to be more reflective of what was going on at home, on the reservations." "One of the big impediments for going on to school," he says, "is that some of the students here, because of housing shortages and other factors, don't have a place to study." But this atmosphere created by the college, acknowledges Littlebear, "is a problem ... students keep coming back here because it is a safe haven." These schools have created another kind of dysfunctional relationship – they're like parents who won't push their kids to leave the nest.

Right now the most educated people on the Indian territories in upstate New York, as elsewhere across the country, work for the tribal government. And often those people moved off the territory to get an education and then were lured back by the tribe's coffers. This model also seems unsustainable, though. Although some Senecas do come back and settle in Buffalo, few middle-class professionals want to actually raise their children on the territories.

It's not only the crime and drugs and poverty. It's also the schools.

Most Seneca kids attend one of four public schools run by the state of New York just off the territories – Silver Creek, Gowanda, Lake Shore, or Salamanca – or a Catholic school called Saint Joseph's, which looks as if it'll be closing soon. The public schools are paid per pupil by the state to educate the Native American population. The school districts all score below the state average on standardized tests. And many parents seem to feel that their students aren't being treated well.

Richard Nephew, a member of the tribal council, tells me that he's particularly upset by the way Seneca kids "are labeled failures even before they can get their feet underneath them." He believes that discrimination is at least in part to blame for the problems. But when I ask whether the tribe has considered increasing its investment in education, Jeffrey Gill, another tribal council member, is somewhat dismissive. He tells me that only a fraction of the kids who leave the reservation actually come back, so it's not clear whether education is a particularly good investment for the tribe.

Gill has two sons, now in their 20s, who attended the Gowanda schools growing up, which is also where Gill went as a kid. He reminisces about their time there, especially their athletic participation. He liked the fact that the principal would come into the locker room after football games. "Both of my sons were presidents of their class . . . I don't have a bad thing to say about it. I really don't. To this day, I enjoyed my education and the leadership roles that both of my sons took when they were there. They played their sports; they played their instruments."

Christina Jimerson, another member of the tribal leadership, whose sons are still in school, is more worried. She tells me that when the local schools' budgets were cut, the Seneca government volunteered to help fund extra "school resource officers" to ensure students' safety. She thinks things "might be getting worse. There is always trouble with [drug use and violence] in any society, but I feel like when I was growing up it was beer and marijuana and now we have kids who are becoming addicted to pills and heroin."

In addition to the security officers, Seneca schools have hired guidance counselors. Seneca students, according to tribal council members, were often getting to their junior or senior year in high school without knowing what courses they'd need to take in order to be college-ready. Jimerson says that the schools were encouraging kids to take easier classes, "not really encouraging them to think about the long term." The guidance counselors are supposed to get involved early on in helping kids pick their classes and ensuring that they're doing their work.

Many Seneca parents also worry that their children aren't getting the help or the professional services they need in school. "It can be intimidating for any parent," says Jimerson. "I felt that way myself going into a meeting about my son.... You have to be their advocate." Jimerson doesn't blame the teachers either, many of whom will tell parents that their kids need more help, even when the school district wants to cut back on services for kids.

What's interesting, though, is that Seneca parents have a choice about where to send their kids. Not only can they, at least for now, make use of the Catholic school in Salamanca, the tribe heavily subsidizes members who send their kids to other private schools. Families typically don't have to pay more than $1,000 per year for private school tuition. Although the best schools in the area are typically in Buffalo or its suburbs – which can be more than an hour's commute for some students – it's interesting that more parents don't take advantage of this option.

Alexis Penhollow, who used to be the education director for the Seneca tribe and now works as the preschool director, believes that the school systems are trying to work with these kids. "I think a lot of what hinders children from taking that next step is that parental involvement piece." Penhollow is working on a doctoral thesis about the question of "why at the higher grade levels parents have a tendency to drop off their involvement in education." She says, "I've looked under the hood and all over the place to try to find an answer, but everybody's reasons are different."

It might have something to do with the fact that the kids who do succeed in high school and go off to college aren't likely to come back.

But Penhollow says that's such a tiny segment of the population that she's not sure it's the real cause. It's much more common for a high-school graduate to go to college and come back after a year.

Penhollow saw this happen a number of times with kids who needed to fill out financial aid forms for college. The tribe would offer to help, she says, but "parents were not always forthcoming with information regarding their salaries, so it left the kids in limbo. Having to deal with that is very stressful." And a lot of students didn't want the hassle.

From a cultural perspective, she says, "we also have a tendency to coddle. We are a small community, and everybody knows each other. We're just a big family." And because most of the parents haven't been to college themselves, they don't know how to prepare students emotionally for the experience. They don't understand what their kids need to do in order to succeed.

It's also true, though, that many of the students are academically unprepared. There have been several attempts to improve the educational prospects for the K–12 students here.

In June 2012, for example, several members of the Seneca Nation submitted a letter of intent to the state of New York saying that they were going to apply to open a charter school on the territory. Using the newly adopted Common Core standards, the Seneca Allegany Charter School, according to the letter, would "provide students with a rigorous education that will uniquely prepare them for success whether they select to pursue a traditional college career or avail themselves of opportunities in advanced technical fields."[8] The proposed chair of the board of trustees was a former president of the nation, with a law degree from Harvard.

According to Penhollow, this was the second time the Seneca applied for a charter. The first was in the 1990s, and she's not sure what happened, but there didn't seem to be enough interest in pursuing it. The application submitted two years ago, she says, was denied because there was no actual facility in which to house the school. This is a problem for many charter schools, which, albeit public schools, are often required to pay for their buildings themselves. In principle, of course, this shouldn't have been a problem for Senecas, who are flush with cash and could presumably have used some of the government-owned land for the purpose.

This was only the latest in a series of failed education ventures, according to Penhollow, who notes that years ago the nation talked about starting its own college. "We've had all these ideas for years. I think it's just implementing them and getting the numbers in order to do this." If it were "the right kind of school," she insists, parents would get behind it. But what would that look like?

A few years ago, there was a proposal to launch a private school on Seneca territory modeled after the Nichols School in Buffalo, probably the best private school in the region. According to Penhollow, the headmaster of the school came to the territory to talk to parents and some of the nation's leaders about the possibility of forming a kind of partnership. The school was going to have a heavy focus on teaching math and science.

But Penhollow says the parents had "concerns." They thought it was "too preppy" or just that it would've been "too much" – that is, too academically rigorous for the students. Parents also worried that it wasn't grounded enough in Native culture and language. Penhollow holds out hope, though, that the Seneca people can start to have "higher expectations" for their kids' education.

But that'll require a change in cultural attitudes toward education.

Lucille Brooks, the SNIEDC administrator for the Seneca tribe, is actually a member of the Mohawk tribe. Shortly after she was born, her mother decided to leave the Mohawk reservation (on the border between Canada and New York) and move to Georgia. Brooks grew up in Georgia and western New York, but always off-territory. Her mother didn't have a high-school education, and she wasn't looking for Brooks to be more educated. But she was looking to remove some of the harmful influences that Brooks might face. "I really believe if I had grown up on the reservation, I probably would have fallen into a lot of the same kinds of trends. There was a lot of drugs and alcohol."

Brooks tells me that her mother thought "what is important is that you're close to Creator, the traditional native way of thinking." Brooks's family had a strong connection to the Mohawk Nation and a strong Native identity. As a child, her grandmother had been sent to a Catholic boarding school against her will and threatened with physical abuse if she used her native language. Hearing about that experience shaped not only Brooks's mother's view of "white people" but also her view of education.

Thus when Brooks told her mother she wanted to go to college, her mother said, "Well, why do you want to do that?" Brooks was fortunate, she says, to have other role models in her life. "At one point in my life, there was a CPA in Georgia I met, and from what I'd seen there was a lot more I could achieve if I became a professional." The woman Brooks met had worked with the governor of Georgia at one point. She "had a beautiful home and everything." And Brooks wanted to be just like her. She went to a community college in North Carolina and then finished her bachelor's degree at Fredonia State in New York.

Her first job was not on a reservation, and she says she was treated poorly there because she was Native. So she got a job working for the Seneca casinos. "I always wanted to come back, because my friends are here and it's like your family."

But being around her friends and family hasn't been easy either. "There are a lot of struggles on territory because of politics here. It's like you're not valued." She says that the things that are important to her, "like keeping a good clean life," aren't valued here. Everything, she says, "depends on who is in politics at the time."

Brooks is optimistic that things will change, however. She tells me that her uncle was once a medicine man. "Back then, it was that knowledge that was so valuable and what carried us through." Now, she says, "it's getting to the point where the transition has to happen for education. Now it's got to be based on facts. When I present to boards [of directors] – in my previous jobs I've presented to doctors, attorneys, and other professionals in the field – it's based on facts."

With the right education and the right role models, though, she feels confident that this transition can occur.

Whenever there's poverty and dysfunction in a community, outsiders want to know whether something inherent in the culture prevents the people in it from getting good jobs, from living clean lives and being productive members of society.

For the most part, the answer is no. Plenty of members of the Seneca Nation have left the territory and gone on to great personal and professional success. The nation now has at its disposal the resources to change some of the facts on the ground. They can lobby and sue federal agencies to get better treatment than they have in the past. There's also a greater social safety net for tribe members who are sick or destitute.

On the other hand, Senecas seem to be learning the hard way that there are limits to what money can buy. By sending out annuity checks, the tribal leadership may be sapping the nation's entrepreneurial spirit. And by adopting the kind of moneymaking strategies that take advantage of various legal loopholes, they encourage the Seneca people to hold fast to a narrative of victimhood. No doubt this was an accurate narrative in the past. But once a tribe makes a billion dollars and then its members find that they don't receive as many preferences in hiring for federal contracts as they used to, it's hard to say this is the same kind of victimhood.

But those payments from casino revenues have encouraged a culture of dependency. This isn't something that's part of Seneca tradition, or any other set of Native beliefs for that matter. But Senecas have responded to economic incentives and disincentives the same way that any other group would.

If direct payments to members of the nation don't seem to be encouraging them in large numbers to save for college or start businesses, what can the money be used for? Education, for one thing. The Seneca people have amassed enough money that they needn't depend on the second-rate public schools in surrounding towns. Although there's general agreement that Seneca students don't do well in these environments – whether because of discrimination or simply because the schools fail to understand their needs – the tribal leadership could do a lot more than just send extra security officers to these districts.

The blame, at least according to Penhollow, lies almost entirely with the parents in the community. It was the parents who didn't push harder for a charter school and rejected a private school alternative when a viable one was offered to them. It's the parents who aren't doing more to get their kids into college and to ensure that they don't return home after a few months. But it's also true that many of the parents don't know just what a successful school can do for their children.

Of all the goals listed on the extensive Seneca Allegany Charter School application, two seem most important: "to raise student achievement first to the level of State average achievement and immediately to a higher level comparable to the highest performing school districts in the region" and "to reverse decades of failure in educating the Native American population, as well as its gross overrepresentation in special education programs," by means of "effective pedagogy that treats culture as a positive influence on learning."[9]

In principle, there's no reason why Seneca culture can't be a positive influence on learning. But the culture that exists on the territory today is holding the nation back.

Ronald Hammonds, of the Lumbee, went to segregated schools as a child and was among those who sued to bring about a single school system in Robeson County. He served on the local school board. "You think you're in pretty good shape until you go visit some of the other schools [in the state]. You realize you need to do better." Even the buildings for the Indian schools were falling apart – "there were still the same leaks there as when I was in school. When it started to rain, you had to move the seats."

Although money might help make things more equitable, he says, "You can't solve the problems in the public schools by increasing the budget every year." He's not sure that charter schools can fix every-thing, but he believes Ben Chavis "can think outside the box. I support his attitudes about charter schools wholeheartedly."

Hammonds himself never got a college degree. "I *attended* six uni-versities. I'll put it like that." When he realized college was not for him, he came home to work on cattle farms. Not everyone has to be college educated, but everyone needs to get a job, he tells me. And the primary and secondary schools aren't preparing students for any kind of job.

Today, he says, schools have more problems to contend with than just money or segregation. "The problem we have today that we didn't have 30 years ago is that you can't let a child run around wild for five years and then expect the school system to do wonders with him. It goes back to the parents and the family. The family unit is eroding, disappearing." A girl at his church recently became pregnant at the age of 12, he tells me. "The parents are supposed to be Christians and all in church. But there's no shame. Our problem really starts at home, and I fault the government for that."

Some Lumbees suggest that this pattern is the inevitable result of a changing economy. Lucy Lowry, the CPA who teaches at nearby Bladen Community College, tells me that just as is true everywhere in the country, "the skills that are required for entry-level positions are now much more refined than they were 25 to 30 years ago, and they are rapidly getting more refined."

When I first sit down with Lowry at one of the picnic tables a few yards from where cattle graze on Chavis's farm, she's insistent that Robeson County's problems are the same as those everywhere. "We aren't unique. This is what's happening all over. This is what's happen-ing in Detroit. It's what's happening in Los Angeles."

But over the course of our conversation, she gets much more spe-cific. For instance, she tells me that "many people here do not have the foundation to adapt to the majority Caucasian economy and don't know how to live in that environment – they are absolutely lost."

She believes that the education system in Robeson County is fail-ing to impart the necessary skills for the 21st-century economy. But they're falling down on the job in other ways too. "We are failing to educate students to be good citizens, to manage their own affairs, to be confident learners – whether they choose agriculture as a profession or teaching, whether they remain here or move out of state."

Lowry, who has also taught math at the secondary level, says that the schools have deteriorated significantly since she was enrolled. This is a theme I hear repeatedly during my time in Lumberton. Even people like Lowry's sister, who went to schools that were still segregated, believe their own education was superior to what their children and grandchildren have received. Sometimes you hear from parents who think there's too much testing in the schools or who believe that the Common Core curriculum has made math incomprehensible to students. But mostly, parents and students complain about a complete breakdown in discipline, a lack of qualified teachers, and poor leadership both among principals and on the school boards.

Also, Lowry says, there is "way too much input from the parents," and not the kind you'd want. "We don't track the kids, because we're trying to satisfy the parents." Parents often complain that the work is too hard, and administrators, according to Lowry, tell the teachers not to assign such difficult material. The teachers are unmotivated, and the schools are so desperate for substitutes that the ones they hire sometimes step out into the hall during class to talk on the phone. Or they eat a meal at their desk while students just watch.

The results of this poor schooling are clear to Lowry in her classroom at Bladen Community College. She says that only about 25 percent of the kids who came to her introductory accounting course were actually prepared to do the work. Most of her students seem to have just been passed through grade after grade without actually learning the material.

Cheryl Beasley, the nursing professor at UNC Pembroke, has had the same experience with nursing students. She has actually been criticized for not admitting a sufficient quantity of Indians to the program at Pembroke, but she says that many local students are simply not meeting the standards. They don't know how to study or how to manage their time, and they don't know how to ask for help from their professors either – particularly if their professors aren't Indian. She says the Indian kids "are more likely to give up." And although some people attribute that to low self-esteem, she thinks Indian students are simply unprepared. "The jump from high school to college for them is massive," she tells me.

When Beasley attended the local schools, they were segregated – there was one school for whites, one for blacks, and one for Indians. Although there were obviously many drawbacks to the arrangement, Beasley notes that she never experienced racism at school. No one is advocating a return to segregation, but other researchers have confirmed Beasley's impression that school integration in the South often resulted in poorer outcomes for racial minorities.

In his book *Acting White*, Stuart Buck paints a stark picture of what black students in one of the newly integrated schools would've faced: a lack of black adult role models, white teachers who were at best condescending and at worst hostile to them, and white peers who tried to keep them out of extracurricular activities. Black students, who were typically behind their white peers academically, were placed in the lowest-performing classes.[10] All evidence suggests that Indians experienced many of the same problems.

The schools in Robeson County today are doing a poor job of educating students in general, but Indians seem to be at the bottom. At Purnell Swett, the high school that most of the Native American students I interview say they are attending or slated to attend, less than a third of students pass English II, and less than an eighth pass Algebra. Among Indians, the percentage of those who pass both is 21 percent, which is lower than for whites and Hispanics but higher than for blacks.[11]

It's hardly any wonder, then, that Beasley finds the pool of students applying to her program to be underqualified and also sees major challenges for those who are admitted to UNC Pembroke. In order to complete the nursing program and move on to a clinical setting, students have to take a math exam each semester and score at 100 percent.

(These are people who are going to be administering medicine, after all, and there's no room for error.) Unfortunately, says Beasley, about 40 percent of the kids who are admitted don't succeed. "They wash out because they can't do the math."

Ben Chavis says the problems at the local schools aren't hard to diagnose. One of the biggest ones is that teachers and principals are hired based on their political connections, not their qualifications. "White people call it nepotism. We call it kinship," he is fond of saying. Indeed, Chavis says that few people in the community are willing to be critical of the schools, even if they know their kids aren't learning much, because the teachers are usually related to them. This is not an uncommon problem in small towns generally, but it seems exacerbated in Indian communities.

At Pine Ridge, too, it's clear that, whatever the quality of education on the reservation, it's the politicians who run things. Not only do they determine what goes on inside the boundaries of the reservation, they're the people who have the most contact with non-Native politicians and the levers of power in Washington.

If Cecilia Fire Thunder, a former president of the Lakota tribe, says that the only thing Lakotas need in order to be more successful is more money, politicians in Washington listen. And it's not only politicians from South Dakota who want to ensure that they have the votes of Native Americans when the next election comes around. This is something that goes all the way to the White House. In 2015, President Obama announced that his budget would include $1 billion for Indians, including a $150 million increase to the Bureau of Indian Education budget. There was another $130 million for school construction, an increase of nearly $60 million over the year before. The plan also included funding for more broadband Internet access in schools.[12]

The truth, though, is that funneling more money into these schools' budgets isn't going to fix their problems. And the money that's already allocated to them is mismanaged to an incredible degree. Just ask Keith Moore. The former director of the Bureau of Indian Education, Moore told me that the BIE was "an inefficient, ineffective, poorly structured bureaucracy." Which was the gist of a memo he tells me he sent to Secretary of the Interior Ken Salazar in 2012. (I made several attempts to obtain the memo through a Freedom of Information Act request, but the BIA has been unresponsive.)

The first problem he sees, and Moore isn't the only one to point this out, is that the Bureau of Indian Education is part of the Bureau of Indian Affairs, not the Department of Education. So whereas most BIA officials are devoted to things like natural resource questions and land development, they also technically oversee education – a subject, notes Moore, they know nothing about. Moreover, the BIA's finances were hard to untangle. "I found it interesting that it was hard to track how the dollars were spent when they were allocated by Congress. I couldn't say with a clear meaning that every dollar appropriated for Indian education was actually being spent on Indian education. The BIA could make that money work differently than [intended]. The BIA had a number of other interests."

And for that matter, it appears that plenty of the money was misspent once it reached the reservation. According to a recent report by the Government Accountability Office, the BIE was aware that 24 schools had misspent $13.8 million in federal Indian School Equalization Program funding on unallowable expenses. But as Rishawn Biddle points out on the blog *Dropout Nation*, "the agency has done nothing to follow-up on the evidence, either by conducting second audits to determine the weaknesses of the schools' financial controls, or to sanction the schools and tribes that operate them for the malfeasance."[13]

But it's not just the money that worries Moore. The Bureau of Indian Education is actually responsible for only a fraction of Indian kids. The majority are educated in state-run public schools. Thanks to No Child Left Behind, there's reliable data on those students. For kids in BIE-run schools, that's not the case, says Moore. "There has to be a quality data and research system developed. We didn't have that."

Tribal leaders and Native school board members say they want to have more power over the schools on the reservation. "They say it's their sovereign right," Moore says, but there needs to be a "tough conversation" about which schools are more successful in educating Indian kids. "But these are conversations people aren't willing to have yet."

Moore was born on the Rosebud reservation in South Dakota and lived there until he was eight. His mother was "full-blood Native" and his father was an Irishman. They met at a dance in a border community. His mother was a school nurse, and his father drove the bookmobile. Though his parents weren't highly educated, he tells me, he and his brothers got a decent education. "The public schools had solid teachers and administrators." Although he's "not saying that the people working in schools today are bad," he assures me, "we have to face the facts and talk about the facts as professionally as we can. We don't have the quality teachers and school leaders we had a generation ago. In science and math and language arts, especially at the middle- and high-school levels, it is tough to find a quality teacher."

When he was director of the BIE, Moore notes, Native Americans would often come to Washington and say "We need more language and culture in the schools." He says that preserving Indian language and culture is "one piece of a 100-piece puzzle. I want language and culture too, but that won't cure our educational dilemma. There are too many other pieces to say 'This is it.'"

A major part of the puzzle, Moore acknowledges, is fixing the family problems plaguing the reservations. "You have broken homes, teen moms, dads not involved, people unemployed." He believes that the "socioeconomic problems are creating school problems." And while some parents know enough to bus their kids 30 miles to a school off the reservation, many simply are unaware of the difference.

But he also sees large segments of the population as "open to educational reform." He thinks that "a number of Native folks would like to see charter legislation." Moore isn't sure that's necessary to achieve

THE NEW TRAIL OF TEARS

the desired ends, since technically BIE schools are free from the control of the local school board. They could actually operate independently, redirect the curriculum – include more language and culture, perhaps. But someone would still have to put some academic measures of success in place, and right now it's hard to imagine anyone on the reservation being able or willing to do this.

CHAPTER FOUR

Walking in Two Worlds

The Weight of Indian Identity

WHEN ANAIYA HOLMAN'S grandmother dropped her off here at Ben Chavis's farm in Lumberton two weeks ago, she was not happy. School had just let out the day before, and Anaiya, who had just finished the fifth grade, didn't want to be stuck in a classroom learning math until July. In fact, she screamed and cried and kicked Chavis in his unmentionables. Chavis was, according to the reports of his other students, unfazed.

This is the fourth year that Chavis has invited kids from Robeson County to come learn math for three weeks at his 200-acre cattle farm in a barn that he has converted into five air-conditioned classrooms. Most of the kids are Lumbees, though a few identify as black or Hispanic (the county is 40 percent Indian).

Some of the boys and girls are happy to be here, but the majority of the 50 or so students between fifth and ninth grade who show up on any given day would rather be doing something else. "That's okay," says Chavis. "This is not supposed to be fun. It's supposed to help them learn."

And, boy, do these kids need help. Students in Robeson County scored an average of 1247 (out of 2400) on the SATs in 2012, more than 200 points below the state average,[1] which was already 40 points below the national average. Students and parents both told me that even if students received Ds and Fs on their report cards, they were sent to the next grade. One parent of a rising fifth-grader told me that the school was giving his son an "okay education." When I later observed the boy in a classroom, he was stumped by flash cards with questions like "11 − 5 = ?"

Several of the students at math camp are living in group homes either temporarily or permanently. Their parents are in some cases incarcerated or too strung out on drugs to care for them adequately. Many other students come from single-parent households.

Chavis does a service to the community merely by providing a disciplined, safe environment for these children, but math camp is much more than that. Between the hours of 8:30 A.M. and 4:00 P.M. every day, the kids get 120 hours' worth of math instruction (interspersed with a few hours of reading, physical education, and lunch). That's equivalent to what they'd get in a *year* at a typical public school.

When students arrive in the morning, they spend the first hour and a half on math. They don't switch classrooms. The classes are all equipped with restrooms and water fountains, so the kids never need to leave. Teachers drill the concepts over and over. They use flash cards, ask children to do problems on dry-erase boards, and have children compete with each other to get answers right. The closest thing these classrooms have to technology is an electric pencil sharpener.

For physical education, the kids at math camp do some calisthenics and run the road around Chavis's farm, just as Chavis himself did half a century ago. It's hot, and they're tired. But they push through. Their teachers are rooting for them, and so are their grandparents.

Students are given about two hours of homework each night. Some of them stay after school to do their homework in a small house where the teachers live. Detention (which can involve anything from washing windows and emptying the garbage to shoveling manure in the barn next door) is given for infractions like tardiness, talking back to teachers, and failing to turn in homework.

The method, as old-fashioned as it sounds, works. In 2001, Chavis took over the failing American Indian Public Charter School in Oakland, California, where his strict standards and no-nonsense attitude earned him the ire of many school administrators but also the respect of many of the low-income neighborhood parents. During Chavis's tenure as principal, AIPCS became one of the highest-performing schools in the state of California, and in 2013 and 2014 it was ranked the number one high school in America, with 100 percent of its students passing at least one AP test.[2] More than three-quarters of its students qualify for free or reduced-price lunch, but all of its graduates are accepted to college, and Chavis helps them pay for tuition.

As Andrew Coulson of the Cato Institute wrote on one of the occasions when Oakland tried to shut down the school, "Low-income black and Hispanic [American Indian Model charter] students actually outperform the statewide averages for wealthier whites and Asians. AIM even outperforms Lowell, one of San Francisco's most respected and academically selective high schools."[3]

Chavis stepped down as principal a couple of years ago, after he was accused of profiting from the school. He doesn't deny the accusation. He leased property to the school – though it was at below-market rates. And he did construction for the school – though his firm was the lowest bidder on the jobs and had done construction for other schools as well. To be honest, though, one would be tempted to give a long leash to anyone who could get such stellar academic results for students stuck in America's worst-performing districts.

Back at the barn, though, everything is charity. Although a few families pay the $300 tuition, the vast majority pay nothing. Some of the mothers offer to cook dinner for the teachers a few evenings in lieu of payment. One of the students actually lives with Chavis and his three children during the week. She's very quiet and doesn't want to be here. When her mother arrives to cook dinner, she's in tears, begging to go home. But her mother can't drive her back and forth every day and wants her to be here. Chavis tells me the mother formerly used drugs and worked as a prostitute but has cleaned up her act. He encourages her to leave her daughter without letting the girl make a scene. It's heart-breaking to watch, but the mother tells me quietly, "It is for the best."

The atmosphere at math camp, one soon-to-be ninth-grader tells me, is "peaceful." Unlike at the school he attends the rest of the year, there's no fighting and no drugs. Fighting and drugs are probably the two biggest reasons that most of these kids' teachers are generally focused on the "troublemakers," as student Lenora Moore puts it.

Because the atmosphere at math camp is so strict and the classes are so small, the teachers Chavis employs generally don't have to deal with such problems. Two of them are graduates of AIPCS. One, a Mexican immigrant, is studying to be a civil engineer at Sacramento State, and the other, who grew up in a home where bullets from rival gangs whizzed through her yard, is studying marine biology at the University of Hawaii.

Chavis also has an old friend who's a retired actuary teaching fifth-grade math. Paul Hanson, a Seattle native, met Chavis on a trip to Mexico about 15 years ago. When I asked what possessed him to come to North Carolina in the middle of June to teach kids who may not want to be here, Hanson says he likes the "integrity and straightforwardness" of the program. "The kids are going to improve, dammit. The kids are going to like math."

Whereas Chavis says he doesn't care whether the kids like it, Hanson is confident they will. "Kids have a natural affinity to mathematics," he tells me. "They like the order. They like the simplicity. And they like the creativity."

Perhaps this sounds counterintuitive, and Hanson is only in his first summer here, so he may be proved wrong. He has a group of children from age 7 to 12, and he's teaching them all third-grade math. "I'm drilling them with flash cards. Once you know these facts, there's nothing more." He says you can know all the basics of math by junior high. "The only thing you do in later years is more complex calculations."

Hanson is aware that the kids he teaches come from difficult conditions at home. But like the other teachers I talk to, he doesn't ask about or encourage them to talk about their home lives. And he doesn't put much stock in the idea that kids need more self-esteem, either. "Math is about being wrong," he tells me. "To learn math, you are constantly wrong all the time." And he says it never ends. "You can pass all your actuarial exams, be paid millions of dollars, and your boss will tell you you're wrong and you can't fall apart."

Perscilla Tovar, the budding marine biologist, tells me that her students often share details of their personal life, "to get attention they are not getting at home." One girl in sixth grade recently announced to the class that her aunt is dating the girl's ex-boyfriend.

Tovar seems to care about the success of her students. It doesn't sound as though she aspires to be a teacher – she says she likes the research aspect of science more than the classroom experience. But she feels a certain debt to Chavis. And it's not just because he's helping her with college tuition. Her older brother was at American Indian Charter before Chavis took over. So Tovar knows what the school was previously like – underperforming and dangerous. When she was in fourth grade, Chavis told her parents he'd pay for her to attend a tutoring program at a place called SCORE to improve her skills before she even entered American Indian in sixth grade. Still, when she started middle school, she was getting a lot of Cs and struggling to complete her work.

But she credits the teachers and Chavis's no-nonsense rules with her success. Her senior year of high school, she was taking seven AP classes – too many, she says in retrospect. But compared with high school, she says, college has been a breeze.

Her first day of math camp was "definitely nerve-wracking," Tovar tells me, while her students work quietly. But she made up lesson plans and followed them and fell into a rhythm. She wasn't intimidated anymore, but "it was frustrating."

She recalls, "I gave them their first test and they didn't do as well as I'd hoped. It makes me question whether I'm a bad teacher. I feel responsible because I'm teaching them. But this is a summer camp, and a lot of these kids don't want to be here. I can't force them to learn." Things have improved even in the past few days. "They're realizing,

'I'm here. I might as well be doing the work.' And it makes me happy when I ask them a question and they just figure it out." Today she asked the kids how many feet were in a mile and one boy actually knew the answer. "I was amazed," Tovar tells me.

Jesse Hinson, one of the other teachers, grew up a few hours away and is now a fine arts major at the University of North Carolina. Her mother met Chavis on a plane one day and, after talking with him, encouraged Hinson to put her mathematical talent to use at the camp.

Hinson doesn't ask the kids too much about where they come from either. She knows that their home lives may not be ideal. "But just because they're not from a nice area or because their school system isn't great doesn't mean they're not as intelligent as any other person in the room. They all know how to do the work. Whether they want to try hard enough is a different matter."

And for what it's worth, the students adore these teachers. Wyatt Bullard, a student who has been coming to math camp for four years, received 59 detention slips his first year. But he eventually decided it was worth it. Every fall, when he returns to school, he finds that he's far ahead of his classmates. He likes the fact that the teachers at math camp are generally young – "They're pretty cool," he tells me. Even Anaiya had softened up by the time I met her. "I want to be a vet," she told me. And when Friday afternoon came around, she asked Chavis whether she could stay at the farm for the weekend.

Noel Evans, who helps out with maintenance at math camp, worked as a custodian at the local middle schools for 17 years and grew up with Chavis. Evans says that parents here "are aware of how bad the public schools are," but they have no other options. One parent, Gloria Gibbs, whose son Nicholas attends nearby Carroll Middle School, says, "This is Robeson County. My hands are tied."

But why don't more parents take advantage of math camp the way Gibbs is doing? Many of the kids at camp have siblings who don't come, for example. When I inquire about these absent brothers and sisters, I'm told they just didn't want to come. For the most part, the kids themselves make the decision.

Gibbs tells me that the problem in the community is the parents. "They are lazy and indigent. They're not going to get up in the morning to bring their children here." Greg Bell, a superior court judge in Robeson County, agrees that "parents don't care." Bell's son teaches at Lumberton High School and says that on parent-teacher conference night, almost no one shows up. Bell's niece and nephew stay with him and his wife during the week so they can attend math camp. Their mother works on the assembly line at the Campbell Soup plant and is divorced from their father. She has had difficulty getting well-paying jobs as a result of not having a college degree.

This year, because school got out so late, math camp has only about half as many students as last year. Only about a third of each classroom is filled. Which annoys Chavis to no end.

Chavis is not a diplomatic man. He regularly uses four-letter words in the company of the kids and employs the phrase "lazy-ass Indians" when a tape recorder is running. The local school administrators are not fans of his. He has been called a racist by members of his own community. And there are many who question his teaching methods. Even if supporters like Ronald Hammonds carry the day, it'll take a long time to change the downward trajectory of this community.

But Chavis wants nothing more than for his community to succeed. He has spent years trying to figure out what makes other ethnic groups rise in this country and why his seems to have ended up at the bottom. A few years ago, he tells me, one of his sisters mocked his focus on education and economic success and accused him of "acting white." "Honey," Chavis told her, "you've got to be more specific. 'Acting white' is not enough. I'm acting Jewish. Or maybe Chinese."

When you ask him why the intense focus on math, Chavis says, "Math is objective. You can trust the numbers." He cites the extraordinary percentage of PhDs in this country that are awarded to foreign students. You don't need to speak good English to succeed. So if Native Americans know math, they can get jobs no matter what. It's a strange

inversion – Chavis sees American Indians as immigrants to the dominant American culture. They're poor, just like immigrants, and starting from behind, so he's proposing strategies that have helped
immigrants succeed.

In looking at the success of other countries in teaching math, he
notes that they're more likely to have longer blocks of time devoted to
the subject. While it's often claimed that kids today don't have the
patience to spend, say, an hour and a half on math, Chavis says the
problem is that "teachers don't want to teach. Schools are designed for
teachers and teachers alone." Indeed, he suggests that it's "teachers
who have short attention spans, not kids."

It's true that as I sit in on the classes, most of the students do seem
to be paying attention. The youngest ones will put their head down on
their desks in the afternoon and take a short nap – something Chavis
actually encourages. But the longer instruction blocks do seem to
allow the teachers to go deep into a particular topic and give the kids
enough practice so that they know how to do the homework.

Chavis is also a big advocate of memorization. "Learning by rote is
one of the best methods." He looks around the farm. "I trained those
cows by rote. Christians go to church on Sunday by rote. Every Sunday
it's the same thing." When asked whether he's worried that the kids
won't like learning, he's characteristically blunt. "I don't give a shit if
they enjoy it. I never think about it."

In addition, he worries that many adults in his community – indeed,
the entire country – spend too much time thinking about what kids
want. "If you listen to kids, if we're going to play that game as parents,
we're going to have a bunch of dumbasses. America is going to be a
third-world country in a hundred years." Referring to one sixth-grader
who gave her grandmother a hard time about coming here, he says, "I
don't care what she wants. I'm the adult. I decide what's good for her."

Many of Chavis's contemporaries recall going to school at a time
when teachers commonly employed corporal punishment, and a few
of them seem to think it's not such a bad idea. Chavis, for his part,

often uses manual labor as detention, but he's not above other methods. He says he'll put kids in the barn with the cows. How is that a punishment? Well, he knows the cows won't harm the kids, but many of the kids don't know it.

Jesse Hinson initially had trouble getting the kids to pay attention to her. She had given plenty of detentions, but it wasn't having the intended effect. Finally she decided to take the large plugs out of her earlobes. It made the kids so uncomfortable to look at her that they started listening. Another time, she just moved one boy's desk right across from her own so that when they did independent work he was under her nose the entire time.

Perhaps the biggest sign of Chavis's confidence in this method of teaching is that his own three children attend not only the charter school in Oakland but also math camp here. "I want them to know they're not better than these people here. They just have more opportunities."

But three weeks a year, Chavis has realized, is not enough opportunity for Lumbee kids. In the fall of 2016, Chavis says, he plans to open a charter school on the farm. He shows me another barn and explains how it could easily be converted to a school building.

There's a charter school not too far away, with a long waiting list. Until recently, North Carolina had a cap of just 100 on the number of charter schools allowed in the state, and in 2011 the National Association of Public Charter Schools ranked the state 32 out of 41, in part because of its low cap and inadequate funding of the schools.[4] But things are looking up. The current governor, Pat McCrory, is "pro-charter," according to Todd Ziebarth, senior vice president for state advocacy and support at NAPCS. Indeed, North Carolina is now 16 on the list, and Ziebarth says there's good reason to think that Chavis could get a charter, given his successes in Oakland.

Ziebarth does say there's cause for concern because of the accusations of financial malfeasance against Chavis. "Whether that's perception or reality, the state will want to vet that stuff." But he says that the state board of education, the body responsible for approving charters, has been particularly sympathetic to applicants in rural counties, since parents there truly have no good options.

Some of the kids at math camp come from mostly working-class families, which have fallen on hard times due to the disappearance of both farming and textile mills from the area. There are few jobs for unskilled workers anymore. But many of the boys and girls here are the *grandchildren* of the middle class. In almost every interview I conduct, I detect a similar pattern. Every extended family has middle-class, working-class, and very poor members. But over and over, it seems as though older family members are the best educated and the most likely to be employed. For a time and for a certain population of Lumbees, education was clearly a priority.

Maxie Maynor went to college, and now his son is studying engineering at UNC Charlotte. But his niece is struggling as a single mother. So Maynor has become a "father figure" to her sons, his great-nephews, bringing them to and from camp and trying to get involved in their education during the year as well. He says the education problem has been present since his son was young. One year, his son didn't have books for the first eight weeks of school. When he asked the principal why not, Maynor was told, "We're waiting to make sure all the kids are enrolled before we order books." He transferred his son to school after school in an effort to get him away from the "chaos" that seemed to reign in the classroom.

Maynor was very active in his son's education, going to school regularly to talk to the teachers and see what was going on. But he says that now principals increasingly tell parents they're not welcome in the schools, something I hear from a number of parents and grandparents.

Nadina Elleby, the wife of an army officer, didn't care what the principals and the teachers thought. Elleby, whose two sons are grown but who volunteered to drive other kids to math camp, tells me that the teachers were thrilled when her kids graduated because they wouldn't have to see her anymore.

Maynor says the leadership of the schools used to be better. Back when his son was in school, a couple of children died in a house fire after their mother, who had no one to watch them, left for work early in the morning. Because it had happened before school hours, one principal decided to open the building at 5:00 A.M. each day so that parents always had somewhere their kids could go. The principal told Maynor, "Those were my children." But Maynor says you don't see that kind of attitude today. "This county is in terrible shape."

For the kids in southeastern Montana, at least, there's an alternative to public schools. The Saint Labre Catholic schools are a group of two elementary schools and one school serving kids in pre-K through 12th grade. Educating about 800 children from the Northern Cheyenne and Crow tribes, the schools are probably the best thing going around here. Named after the French saint, Benedict Joseph Labre, Saint Labre was founded in 1884 by a small group of Catholic Ursuline Sisters from Toledo, Ohio. The mission actually predates the reservation. A local homesteader contacted his bishop about the plight of the Northern Cheyenne, who had been forced off their land by settlers and were wandering what's known as the Tongue River Valley. The bishop, John Brondel, purchased some land and put out a call for priests and nuns to come work with the Northern Cheyenne. Three Ursuline Sisters showed up, and for many years they lived, worked, and prayed in a three-room cabin on the land. In the years afterward, the mission underwent great hardship – almost closing altogether in the 1950s due to a lack of funding.[5]

Today, Saint Labre runs a variety of programs for the community, including group homes for children whose parents can't care for them, elder services, day care, and job training.

But Saint Labre's most significant contribution to tribe members' lives has been its schools. They're technically under the auspices of the Great Falls–Billings diocese, but they receive no money from it. They also don't take most forms of funding from the federal government. The school's budget is drawn entirely from donations. And the tuition is free.

Saint Labre's main campus – which serves 500 students – is located about 125 miles southeast of Billings. There's no place for visitors to stay except the school itself, in bare-bones guest rooms that look as though they were last renovated in the 1970s. There's no television, and students and visitors alike are blocked from accessing social networking sites or watching streaming videos. Cell-phone service is spotty at best.

The town has a video store, a couple of bars, a diner, and a small supermarket – with a well-stocked beer aisle but a paltry selection of meat and produce. Saint Labre teachers who live on campus often drive to Billings on the weekends to do their grocery shopping.

The campus itself is sprawling, with mostly single-story buildings. It is neatly kept, and the classrooms are airy and cheerful. On the opposite end of campus from the church – a pyramid-like structure with a giant cross that looks as if it has been sent crashing into the side of the building – is the cultural arts center, where students have the option of studying a native language – either Crow or Cheyenne – as well as drumming and beadwork.

The school has a dual mission – "To proclaim the Gospel of Jesus Christ according to Catholic Tradition by providing quality education which celebrates our Catholic faith and embraces Native American cultures, primarily the Northern Cheyenne and Crow Tribes, so that Native American Individuals and communities of Southeastern Montana are empowered to attain self-sufficiency."[6] Ultimately, Saint Labre's function is to give Native children a decent education, something they're not getting at the public schools on the reservation.

At Saint Labre, the dropout rate is only around 1 percent. And each year since 2010, 100 percent of its graduating seniors have been accepted to college. Not all of them have gone on immediately to attend – 83 percent in 2010 – but the preparation provided by Saint

Labre for whatever they want to do is clearly superior to the alterna-tives.[7] (Of course, no good deed goes unpunished. In 2005, Saint Labre schools were sued by one of the tribes, which wanted a share of the funds that they had raised.[8] Never mind that the money was being used to educate the tribe's own children.)

Not only do a much higher percentage of Saint Labre graduates go to college compared to graduates of public schools both off and on the nearby reservations, Saint Labre ensures that students understand the benefits of going to college. For one thing, Saint Labre exposes its stu-dents to life off the reservation. They attend math competitions in Denver and college preparatory programs at Princeton and Dart-mouth. They meet kids from different backgrounds and start to under-stand the doors that are open to them if they can manage to get a decent education.

Saint Labre even partners with Mount Saint Mary's College in Maryland to offer one graduate per year free college tuition – Saint Labre pays half of the cost, and Mount Saint Mary's pays the other half.

Kurri Harris received this year's scholarship to Mount Saint Mary's College. Harris is part Crow and part Cheyenne. Her mother is an EMT, and her father is a heavy equipment operator. Her parents sent Harris and her siblings here because the local public school wasn't safe enough. Harris says the biggest difference she notices is that the kids at Saint Labre turn in their homework on a regular basis. That doesn't happen in Lame Deer. Harris says she plans to study physical therapy and would like to come back to the reservation to work someday.

Some of the kids I interview at Saint Labre tell me they have friends who have dropped out and gone back to public school. "This place is hard, and they make you wear uniforms," says one middle-school girl. By which she means khakis and a polo shirt. Yet the school's paternalistic policies – a dress code, after-school hours set aside for homework, living in dormitories, and teachers who demand parental involvement – are in part responsible for its success. At other schools, kids are simply allowed to make their own choices.

Winfield Russell, of the Northern Cheyenne tribal council,

attended Saint Labre, but he told his kids they could decide where they wanted to go. He compares it to buying his son sneakers. "I used to buy his basketball shoes. I used to buy him what I wanted him to wear. And here I finally realized, you know, they went to school [at Lame Deer] because he liked it and they wanted him to go to school here."

Ivan Small, the director of the Saint Labre Catholic schools, has a hard time understanding why the parents he deals with let their kids – sometimes as young as eight – make decisions about their own education. But he has seen firsthand the complete disintegration of the Indian family. It's not just "babies raising babies." A number of his students are wards of the Bureau of Indian Affairs. Some are being raised by older siblings. Their home lives are chaotic – riddled with drugs and alcohol and abuse of all sorts.

Their lives aren't much different from the lives of kids in the South Bronx or Compton. The dysfunction, the culture of dependency – it's all there. But there are differences between rural poverty and urban poverty. Right now in our worst inner cities there are parents begging for scholarships to Catholic schools, waiting for charter school lotteries, doing whatever they can to give their children a chance at a better life. Why aren't the communities around Saint Labre doing the same? Saint Labre, like other Indian Catholic schools, is regularly dismissed in casual conversation by community leaders. Why are there empty seats in all of its classrooms? Why are there extra beds in its dormitories?

For one thing, parents on the reservation don't seem to be aware that things could be better for their children. Parents in the South Bronx – even if they just get on the subway occasionally – are aware of people dressed in suits going to middle-class jobs. When you're 100 miles from Billings, Montana, there's no such realization. When Small takes kids from his school on field trips – to math competitions or to visit colleges in Washington, D.C., the kids are stunned. They might as well have gone to another planet.

But there's also this: many of the parents don't want their kids to leave. It's almost the opposite of an immigrant mentality. If you spend enough time interviewing working-class parents who have recently come to America from the Dominican Republic or Mexico or Poland or Russia or Italy, you'll understand that as much as they love their children, they aren't hoping that as adults, their children won't move to a nicer neighborhood. For them, the whole point of coming to this country was to move up socially and economically. Most Native American parents don't share this attitude.

It may seem surprising to outsiders that the kids who do go to college frequently return to the reservation after they graduate. These kids feel a sense of familial obligation – though many have trouble finding work. Karl Little Owl attended Mount Saint Mary's after Saint Labre. When he returned to the reservation, the only jobs available were in tribal government. So now he spends his days applying for grants from the federal government. "My push is always looking for opportunities where there are not a lot of strings attached."

More commonly, I hear from a number of residents, students attempt college but quickly return. They get homesick or feel as though they don't fit in at college. Saint Labre now has an administrator whose sole job is to keep up with these college kids and make sure they're getting the support they need.

It's odd that Richard Littlebear, president of Chief Dull Knife College, is dismissive of the efforts of Small and the Saint Labre School. Littlebear worries that Saint Labre "can pick who they want." It's true that Saint Labre doesn't accept kids with severe disabilities, but by offering free tuition and transportation and even boarding facilities to almost any student on the reservation, Saint Labre can't be said to be creaming off the better students. Littlebear goes on to say, "One of the characteristics of all parochial schools was that they really promoted their own agendas, which were Christian agendas of a missionary type." The public schools, on the other hand, were "parent-driven in educating Native American students."

Yet Saint Labre is run by a "full-blooded" Indian who makes a point of celebrating Indian customs and teaching Native languages, something fewer and fewer of the adults know anyway. And most Indians are Christians, as outsiders might be surprised to learn.

Churches – from Pentecostal to Baptist to Catholic – dot the reservation landscape. The Crow legislature recently passed a "Resolution of the Crow Tribal Legislature to Honor God for His Great Blessings upon the Crow Tribe and to Proclaim Jesus Christ as Lord of the Crow Indian Reservation."[9] And a banner with similar language hangs in the legislative building.

When I probed Littlebear further about Saint Labre in particular, he says, "This is what I've heard. I just don't know that much."

And so it goes. Even the people on the reservation who should be most interested in the educational success of Cheyenne and Crow students – members of the tribal council, the president of the local college – have little interest in the one school that seems to be giving students the knowledge and preparation they need to lift up themselves and their families. It doesn't seem to faze Small. But at this point, nothing does.

Tribal leaders and parents are often suspicious of non-Indians and of what might happen to their children if they leave the reservation. They're even suspicious of Saint Labre because of the terrible history in the United States (and even more so in Canada) of removing Indian children from their homes and re-educating them at private and parochial boarding schools.

These residential schools were symbols of everything that was wrong with Indian policy in the United States and Canada for much of the past 200 years. The mere mention of these now-closed schools still makes many Native people shiver. The schools were paternalistic, abusive, and unrelenting in their goal to erase tribal culture. Under threat of physical abuse, the schools forced children to forgo their native languages and customs, cut their hair, and effectively separate from their families and their own history.

Launched in the late 19th century, some of these schools were run by religious groups. But the Bureau of Indian Affairs also started some of its own, modeled on the Carlisle Indian Industrial School in Pennsylvania. Founded by Captain Richard Henry Pratt in 1879, Carlisle was supposed to "Americanize" Indians.

In his address to the Nineteenth Annual Conference of Charities and Correction in 1892, Pratt set out his plan for "civilizing" the tribes to the west. He argued that efforts to educate Indians – carried out mostly to that point by missionaries – had been largely fruitless because the missionaries had let Indians largely keep their own ways and stay separate from white people. The Carlisle School, and the 150 or so boarding schools that followed it, had a different model. Pratt explained:

> It is a great mistake to think that the Indian is born an inevitable savage. He is born a blank, like all the rest of us. Left in the surroundings of savagery, he grows to possess a savage language, superstition, and life. We, left in the surroundings of civilization, grow to possess a civilized language, life, and purpose. Transfer the infant white to the savage surroundings, [and] he will grow to possess a savage language, superstition, and habit. Transfer the savage-born infant to the surroundings of civilization, and he will grow to possess a civilized language and habit. These results have been established over and over again beyond all question; and it is also well established that those advanced in life, even to maturity, of either class, lose already acquired qualities belonging to the side of their birth, and gradually take on those of the side to which they have been transferred.[10]

When I interviewed people at Wounded Knee in South Dakota, it became increasingly apparent that the former Holy Rosary Mission school left scars on many of its residents. Founded 125 years ago as the Holy Rosary Mission by the Jesuit order and the Sisters of Saint Francis of Penance and Christian Charity, Holy Rosary – like many Catholic schools on reservations – saw its task as to bring the Catholic faith, and some might say the dominant white culture, to residents of the reservation. Even after it changed its name to Red Cloud in the 1960s to honor the great Lakota chief and the school's Indian heritage, many continued to see it as a vehicle for the subjugation of Indian culture.

Cecilia Fire Thunder of the Lakota tribe, who attended Red Cloud through 10th grade, tells me, "They were colonizing us and trying to make us more like them." People, she says, "tell me I speak such great English and they ask me where I went to school. I refuse to answer questions about Red Cloud. I am learning to let go of the pain and damage they inflicted on me."

And it's not just her. As the superintendent of the school, Ted Hamilton, tells me, Red Cloud "has a kind of Dr. Jekyll/Mr. Hyde thing" going on. "Red Cloud has done really great things, particularly in the last 30 years." But "it's got [a century] years of doing really bad things to Indian people – horrible things to Indian people." Hamilton is white and grew up in Illinois. After earning his master's degree in library science, he found that library jobs were scarce, so he applied to be the archivist at Oglala Lakota College. "They didn't have archives," he clarifies. "They had boxes of stuff." So Hamilton moved to Pine Ridge to help them create an archive and train people on the reservation to keep it themselves. He eventually received a grant from the Ford Foundation to do this work for other tribal colleges as well.

Hamilton married a Lakota woman who already had six children. He then went on to work in different areas of education – he helped with technology and libraries and worked at various local schools. He has been at Red Cloud for 29 years now, and "I'll be here until they bury me," he tells me, laughing.

A year after he was married, his oldest son was going to be a freshman, and Hamilton suggested that they send him to Red Cloud. His wife, who had attended Red Cloud, wasn't excited but agreed. Hamilton recalls the first time he really understood the issue:

> *I remember the first parent-teacher conference. We got up to that entryway over there and she said, "Stop the car." I stopped the car. She burst into tears. And so, here I am with my relatively young wife, new wife, and she's crying like crazy. I'm like, "What is going on?" She says, "I swore I would never set foot on this campus again. I had to board here. My parents left me here."*

She said, "They wouldn't let us speak Lakota." She's a full-blood, and Lakota was her first language. She said, "They wouldn't let us speak our language. This is an oppressive place, and yet somehow I let you talk me into letting my son go to school here." I had to do the parent-teacher conference alone. She never left the car.

By the time a year went by, she had gotten used to it and managed it. The other three boys that we had, who are our youngest three, went to school here; she was much more comfortable. But there is that history here, and there are people who still remember the boarding schools as being both positive and negative. I've known many Native people [who] say, "The boarding schools were a great experience for me," and others who will say it was horrendous. It kind of depends on who you talk to and what their experience was.

In Canada, the residential schools were funded by the federal government, but in most cases they were administered by religious organizations. According to an account by CBC News, a division of the Canadian Broadcasting Company: "Initially, about 1,100 students attended 69 schools across the country. In 1931, at the peak of the residential school system, there were about 80 schools operating in Canada. There were a total of about 130 schools in every territory and province except Newfoundland, Prince Edward Island and New Brunswick from the earliest in the 19th century to the last, which closed in 1996. In all, about 150,000 First Nation, Inuit and Métis children were removed from their communities and forced to attend the schools."[11] (Métis are people of mixed European and First Nation ancestry.)

Manny Jules attended the residential school In Kamloops, British Columbia, but didn't have to live there – which, he acknowledges, means that he had a different experience from many of his peers. "I was never sexually abused or physically abused. I never got the strap or got beat up." Perhaps it was because he came from a family of tribal leaders: his great-grandfather was a chief, and his father was on the tribal council.

Jules attended residential schools until seventh grade and then went to the local "white" school in Kamloops. In some ways, he recalls, that was harder for him. "When I got to that school, there were still some places in town Indians couldn't go." He was mocked for being Indian and mocked for being poor. But his parents wouldn't let him drop out, emphasizing the importance of education. It's the same message he gives his own daughter: "You have to be able to look after yourself and not depend on anyone."

The office where Jules works isn't far from the house where he grew up, which is about the size of this workspace. The office is a study in contradictions. The large hardwood-framed windows, the oak conference table, and the imposing desk in the corner all date to the late 19th century, when this building was part of a residential school for Indians that Jules attended.

But Jules's office is also decorated with important pieces of tribal history. Otter pelts and buckskin clothing adorn a proud-looking mannequin. The otter is decorated with red ochre, Jules tells me, which was used before the advent of beading. Photos and proclamations line the walls, a combined accounting of Jules's own history, including his time as chief of the Kamloops band, and the history of the Aboriginal Peoples of British Columbia. When the residential school closed, many wanted to destroy this building – even burn it to the ground – but Jules wanted to make it the headquarters for the Kamloops band leadership.

Whether or not it affected Jules personally, the abuse and its effects on the community as a whole are hard to escape. "The majority of the kids I went to school with are dead," he says, "because of the experience they had, the abuse, the separation [from their families and communities]."

It was only a few years ago that, working with leaders of Anglican, Catholic, and other churches, the Canadian government developed a plan to compensate members of the affected communities for this sad chapter in the country's history. A fund of $1.9 billion (Canadian) was set aside for payment to anyone who had attended these schools, of which $1.6 billion has been paid out. Those who had suffered sexual abuse or serious physical abuse could press their claims separately.[12]

In 2008, Prime Minister Stephen Harper issued an apology on behalf of the Canadian government for the residential school system, and leaders of all the churches involved have done something similar. The Catholic Church, which was responsible for educating three-quarters of the students in the system, was the last to do so. In 2009, Pope Benedict expressed his "sorrow" to a delegation from Canada's Assembly of First Nations for the abuse and "deplorable" treatment that First Nation students suffered at Catholic residential schools.[13]

Still, for most members of First Nations who are Jules's age or older, the residential schooling system was the defining experience of their lives. As a result, they're wary of any change in federal policy, particularly anything that seems as if it might be another attempt at assimilation. They're not happy with the status quo – members of First Nations are doing abysmally by every economic and social indicator – but potential solutions are met with great skepticism.

So it's not surprising that, even today, when outsiders come to teach at traditional public schools on reservations, community members are suspicious. The presence of Teach for America fellows is one of the biggest sources of conflict in reservation schools. At Wounded Knee, the federally funded turnaround team fired all 10 of its teachers and told them to reapply for their jobs. Only two made the cut. The other eight were from Teach for America. And this isn't a coincidence. Alice Phelps, the newly installed principal, explained why the TFA corps members didn't belong at Pine Ridge. "None of them were asked back," she tells me, "because they'd have to be highly qualified. We wanted highly qualified teachers who had experience and could manage our students and also work on strategies to bring them up."

The battle over Teach for America has intensified across the United States in the past couple of years, with union-backed protest movements taking hold at universities and with members of the teaching establishment criticizing the group in op-ed pieces and on cable news. But nowhere is TFA facing more opposition than in Indian communities.

On the surface, welcoming Teach for America should be a no-brainer. TFA is obviously selective: for the 2014–15 school year, it had 50,000 applicants and accepted about 5,300 of them. Over 10,000 corps members now work in 50 urban and rural districts, and they come from the best schools in the nation. One in five has a degree in science, math, technology, or engineering[14] – the areas our public schools are most deficient in. Corps members typically commit to a two-year stint at an underserved school, attending a training camp over the summer to learn classroom management and continuing their professional development while in the classroom.

So why the objection to TFA's presence? Or more to the point: if you're a principal who doesn't seem to have a grasp of first-grade math, how can you fire young men and women with Ivy League degrees who want to spend at least two years of their lives working for next to nothing to help your kids succeed?

A typical critic of TFA is Mark Naison, a professor of African American Studies at Fordham University, who explained in the *Washington Post* why he won't let TFA recruit from his classes: "Until Teach For America becomes committed to training lifetime educators and raises the length of service to five years rather than two, I will not allow TFA to recruit in my classes. The idea of sending talented students into schools in impoverished areas, and then after two years encouraging them to pursue careers in finance, law, and business in the hope that they will then advocate for educational equity *really* rubs me the wrong way."[15]

Critics also claim that TFA corps members lack traditional certification from the states where they teach and are thus less able to manage underprivileged kids. But a quick walk through any inner-city public school would make you wonder exactly what education-school grads have been learning.

Finally, critics believe TFA corps members are just too white. They don't always put it that way, but for years they've accused TFA of having a "savior" mentality. In the fall of 2014, Teach for America responded directly to this criticism, boasting of the "most diverse" corps in its history, according to a press release, with 50 percent of its teachers identifying as people of color. "We're proud that our incoming corps is more diverse than it's ever been," said Elisa Villanueva Beard, the group's co-CEO. "We know that teachers from all backgrounds can have a meaningful impact on their students' trajectories."[16]

But how meaningful is it? Jay Greene, who heads the Department of Education Reform at the University of Arkansas, notes that, when compared to other possible improvements, "The benefit [of having same-race teachers] is tiny." Moreover, these gains are "zero sum," meaning that students who aren't the same race as the teacher don't get the benefit. So are we supposed to segregate our classrooms to maximize this effect?

Anyway, the real question isn't how to improve the diversity of the teacher corps but how to improve teacher quality: we need more teachers who help their students perform well.

The teachers Phelps hired at Wounded Knee to replace the TFA corps members were largely lured from other schools on the reservation by offers of about $10,000 more a year. Whether these teachers are more qualified than TFA corps members remains to be seen, but since there's a massive teacher shortage on the reservation, it's hard to imagine that this strategy will work in the long term. Even if every school were "turned around," it would just be like rearranging deck chairs on the *Titanic*.

Meanwhile TFA continues to fill the void. Robert Cook leads the Native Alliance Initiative for Teach for America. Cook's parents both grew up on Pine Ridge, but he was raised in a small town outside of Rapid City. They were the only Indian family in town. He went to the local public school and then went to Brigham Young University to play baseball. His older sister joined the Mormon Church at the urging of local missionaries, and later Cook did too. After college, he came home and taught at a variety of local schools. He tells me he never had to have an interview "because there was never any competition for teaching jobs."

Cook, who has received numerous teaching awards, including a Milken Educator Award, joined TFA in 2010. He's a gruff man and somewhat suspicious of the media. But he has a good handle on the educational problems plaguing Pine Ridge and other reservations. The biggest challenge "is human capital." "How can you advance students in math and reading if you don't have certified math and science teachers? How can you push students if you don't offer advanced placement courses?" he asks. "Our students have every capability and every desire to do good, but if you don't have the investment in the classroom with boots on the ground," it amounts to nothing.

How do you get qualified people to come to Pine Ridge? Every school on the reservation is scrambling for teachers. But the tribal school – Oglala Lakota College – doesn't even offer a degree in secondary education. So you need to recruit from off the reservation.

In addition to salaries being low (which is true for teachers in most rural areas), teachers have difficulty finding housing and even receiving health care. Most of the schools house their teachers in run-down trailers. It takes a particular kind of person to want to live here for two years, let alone do a longer stint as the critics of TFA are suggesting.

To be blunt, teachers who come here have to really want to be here. But tribal leaders seem nevertheless intent on insulting their abilities and even their motives. Fire Thunder tells me, "They're not adequately prepared. We have some enthusiastic ones, but they have a different mind-set." She notes that many of them "are majoring in something else" besides education and that this is a problem. Yet research suggests that teachers who major in the subject matter they'll be teaching are significantly more effective than those with education degrees. When I ask Fire Thunder about the teachers fired from Wounded Knee, she says dismissively, "I don't think any of them were Native."

But truth be told, Fire Thunder is even skeptical of the Native teachers educated in universities off the reservation. "They are too white. They think Western. They have bought into the Western way of thinking lock, stock, and barrel. They look down on us. They don't value their culture. They don't understand anything about their culture."

WALKING IN TWO WORLDS

Does that hold true for Kiva Sam, the woman who runs South Dakota recruitment for TFA? Fire Thunder doesn't want to talk specifically about her.

Sam's grandparents raised her on Pine Ridge. Her grandmother, who had a degree from MIT in urban and rural planning, had worked on cleaning up the reservation after the Badlands were used as a bombing range during World War II. Her grandfather, who had attended Harvard, had a law degree and an education degree. He was a member of the Chocktaw tribe from Mississippi but helped rewrite the constitution here on Pine Ridge.

Sam says she was "always considered the smart student" at Wounded Knee, and in retrospect, one of her principals said, they let her slip through the cracks. Her freshman year in high school, she got a scholarship to Proctor Academy, a prep school in New Hampshire. But like so many kids who leave this tight network of extended family on the reservation, Sam was homesick. She was also severely underprepared – having no idea how to study for exams, she tells me. She left halfway through the year and returned to attend Bennett High School, a majority Indian school just off the reservation.

But those few months away changed things for her. "It was very alienating. . . . A lot of my peers thought, 'Oh, you're acting like a white girl now.' It made me feel very ostracized." She had trouble figuring out where to fit in at Bennett, which had both white kids and Indian kids. "For a lot of non-Native students there were certain expectations, but for a lot of the Native students it was okay to sleep [in class]. It just didn't seem like there was a lot of effort being put into ensuring that they were succeeding." Sam was smart, but she was wary of being branded "white" again.

She skipped a lot of her classes during that year but got As anyway. Then, in her sophomore year, she became pregnant. She decided to keep the baby, and her life seemed to take on a renewed sense of purpose. "I was going to school every day on time, getting my work done." She took classes at Lakota College in addition to her high-school classes. Her mother offered to help care for her son, but Sam nevertheless had to start working to support him – 25 hours a week – in addi-tion to going to school. She doesn't mention the child's father.

Perhaps because of her family background, Sam planned all along to go to college. During the summer before her junior year of high school, she attended a program at Princeton University called Leader-ship Enterprise for a Diverse America. LEDA helps underprivileged kids prepare for the college admissions process, offering them writing preparation, standardized test instruction, and leadership training. Sam applied to Dartmouth College and was admitted.

But then what? She originally thought she would bring her son with her to school, but it quickly became clear, she said, that it wouldn't be feasible. There were students who had children, but they were mar-ried and living in graduate student housing. There wasn't a big single-mother population on campus. "There weren't a lot of support systems in place to ensure that students who were nontraditional parents could succeed in that environment," Sam tells me.

And so Sam made the difficult decision to leave her son at home. While in school, she worked almost full-time to send money home for him. She bought his clothing, and, she tells me, "Sometimes I had to help my mom with the electricity bills and water bills."

Having decided to major in government, Sam was considering law school, but she wondered whether it was just because "that's what my grandpa did and that's what was expected of me." After all her time away from home, she says, "I just felt like I needed to reconnect to my people and my community." She talked to a Teach for America recruiter and decided to apply. Sam had been taught by someone from TFA during school and remained in contact with her over the years.

Her teacher was a Chocktaw from Oklahoma, and Sam says she was very honest about her experience, which began in 2004. "Back then, there were no systems in place to help ensure that corps mem-bers of color were succeeding, corps members who shared the same backgrounds as their students." She felt TFA "was representative of a dominant society of white kids."

Indeed, the notion that TFA was a bastion of white privilege was so pervasive that Sam almost decided to go serve in the Navajo Nation instead. "I wanted to work with Indian kids, but I didn't want to feel out of place again." She didn't want people to think of her as the white girl again. Finally she decided, though, that she needed to be at home. She went to teach social studies at Little Wound High School. (I had arranged to visit Little Wound during my time at Pine Ridge, but a bomb threat closed the school for several days.)

When I ask Sam whether she felt like an outsider at Little Wound because she was a part of TFA, she says most people didn't know that she was with TFA. Once they found out, her colleagues were fairly accepting. But it's telling that Sam didn't advertise her TFA affiliation. "It's a very divided community on this issue, I think, for good reason," she says.

As a recruiter for TFA, Sam says that she's very careful not to recruit people with "that savior mentality ... like 'Oh, I'm going to help save these kids, these Indian children." Instead, she says, she's looking for someone "coming here because you want to provide something that they're currently not getting."

When I ask her to clarify this point, she says, "I would want some-one who is open, who is willing to feel uncomfortable, because you're probably coming from an area where you're the majority and now you're going to be the minority." It's hard to imagine people applying to come to a reservation in South Dakota if they're not willing to feel uncomfortable, but if Sam says such people exist, well, she should know.

Joshua Menke teaches math at the Crazy Horse School in the town of Wanblee. Menke is actually in his fourth year here – his TFA stint ended two years ago. Born in South Dakota but raised in rural Min-nesota, Menke had Native friends growing up and in college, but he's not Native himself. Most of his experience in elementary school was in a multi-grade classroom, and he has given a lot of thought to the particular challenges of educating kids in a rural setting.

Menke teaches 9th- through 12-grade math and has to do different preparation for each class for each day. The job definitely presents challenges. "There are not a lot of resources. It's been 20 years since we had a high-school football team," Menke says. But he seems used to it. "What's cool is that this year my current seniors I've taught every year since they were freshmen." Each year, he's torn between trying to push ahead with the curricula they're supposed to learn and building the basics that they never got in the early grades. The classes are small, and though Menke is not a commanding presence, he knows each student's strengths and weaknesses, ensuring that they all pay attention and answer questions.

Menke has thrown himself not only into his job but also into the community. He lives in a trailer near the school, and during the summers he participates in local sports leagues. "There is a softball league that happens in town and [there are] powwows all the time. When they see people here for the summer, they realize you're not just here teaching or working. You're inside the community."

A couple of years ago, nearby Badlands National Park was looking for people to help with their internship programs, and Menke applied. Last year, he directed the program and oversaw five students from Crazy Horse in an intern ranger program. "Some of it is learning to man the desk and interact with visitors, but they are also shadowing people doing paleontology." They did field trips and hiking and camping and traveled to New York City as ambassadors for the program.

When Sam says "I want people who are truly passionate about providing opportunities to students," it's hard to imagine anyone who fits the bill better than Menke. Despite his non-Native status, the community seems to have embraced him.

Jim Curran, the executive director of TFA in South Dakota, says this story isn't at all unusual. He acknowledges that the organization "is sometimes looked upon favorably and sometimes not." But he suggests that those who are skeptical are often those least familiar with it. "If their kid actually has a Teach for America teacher – that's probably the biggest changing point." In August, there were 45 vacant teaching slots on Pine Ridge, and parents are happy to see that many of them have been filled by qualified instructors. In October during my visit, there are still at least 10 vacancies.

Curran says he has received a kind welcome from the communities here. "I think what surprised me more was the fact that some people were willing to take me under their wing, invite this random white dude to a birthday party or a ceremony. I feel like I really got lucky."

Sam says that part of the challenge is having TFA corps members understand the goals of students and parents here. "At Teach for America, there is this push for college, college, college. And that's important, but at the end of the day, some of our students want to do mechanics. It's not a four-year degree, but it is higher education, and if a student wants to do that, then as teachers we need to ensure that we're helping that student actualize his dreams."

Sam's point is well taken, but it seems as though the issue here isn't what kind of higher education kids will go on to but whether they'll finish high school at all. Sam tells me that during her first year teaching, the average daily attendance was 60 percent. She would try calling the homes of kids who were regularly absent, but "school is the last thing on their minds. They're not in that zone."

There are truancy laws on the reservation, but they go unenforced. "How are we assuring that we are accountable in all aspects?" Sam asks. There's a limit to what educators can do, she says, because "our tribal government is one of the most dysfunctional tribal governments in the United States." She also complains about the "deep family politics" involved in decisions at the school level.

When she was teaching a couple of years ago, she had one student who wasn't showing up to class or doing the work. She kept his mother in the loop, and when it came time for graduation, Sam told her, "He has not been here. I told you that." A member of the student's family was on the school board, and the principal told Sam to pass him anyway. "We had a very tense conversation. I told him, 'If you want to pass him, you can, but I'm not going to. Because what you're doing is what's wrong with the reservations. We're not teaching students that they have to show up to earn something, that they actually have to put the effort and the work in.'"

Sam lost the battle. Her student, like so many others, graduated anyway. The effects of such actions, she says, are far-reaching. "If you look at Oglala Lakota College, most of their entering freshmen are working at below a 10th-grade level. They're not prepared. But then in college they're getting pushed through because it looks better to graduate more students than to graduate students who are prepared." And there's no real check on such policies, because the students who graduate don't then go on to compete for jobs in a real market. If they find employment, it's with the tribal government or at one of these schools. And then the cycle repeats.

Sadly, Sam says the situation has gotten worse. Because her own family was deeply involved in Indian politics in the '60s and '70s, she became familiar with the landscape. Of the American Indian Movement, she notes, some of the leaders didn't have college degrees, but they deeply valued education, if for no other reason than they wanted to understand "the legal aspects of the U.S. pertaining to us."

Sam hastens to add that the fact that kids today are being raised by teenagers is not helping. Yes, she realizes that she was part of this epidemic, but during her first year of teaching at a school of 300, there were 17 pregnancies. The effects of this are staggering.

And there's only so much a school can do to combat these distractions. Parents have to take responsibility too. Curran believes that a big part of TFA's role on the reservation is to encourage greater involvement in education. "A key challenge of education reform in Native communities is that the voices of parents, just the everyday parents, are very commonly left out of the solutions and the conversations that are happening in the state house or the Bureau of Indian Education."

Menke has found that "parents care a lot about their students' education, but there is also a different relationship to the educational infrastructure in general." Largely because of the boarding-school experience, "There is definitely some mistrust." Sometimes that mistrust works to prevent students from going away to college as well. But Menke says that, more often than not, the kids feel an obligation to stay home. "A lot of students really are involved in their siblings' lives." In some cases, Menke has encouraged them to at least consider attending nearby Black Hills State University so they can be close to home but still continue their education.

This obligation of young people to stay home to care for others comes up frequently in my interviews. The Ruth Danley and William Enoch Moore Fund was launched by a teacher who received a bequest from a relative. Bruce Bickel, who helps administer the $16 million fund,[17] travels around the country looking for ways both large and small – such as paying for school buses, school kitchens, teacher bonuses, and scholarships – to improve Indian education. But Bickel is concerned about the other factors keeping kids from graduating. In some cases, he says, boys will leave school at 16 to go to work fighting forest fires. Girls will drop out to take care of their older relatives or their younger siblings.

Curran realizes that for many families there's a delicate balance going on here. And TFA can't just come in and tell all the students that they're going to go to college. But he's definitely irritated by community leaders who say that encouraging kids to go to college is antithetical to the tribe's goals. In the name of "tribal self-determination," he says, they'll "decide in seventh grade if it's right for a kid to be going to college or not."

He says it's teachers' responsibility to make sure that kids "can determine what they want to do, and they should have the same options that any kid from the South Bronx or the suburbs of Minneapolis has, and that means they have to be prepared." So TFA has settled on both of those things – college readiness and tribal self-determination. The latter will allow kids to "make decisions aligned with their own values and their own culture."

In general, he says that parents complain more about the schools' underperformance than about their children being taught by people with a "savior" mentality. "People are frustrated with expectations not being high enough or that their kid is not being pushed enough."

But they also don't understand what's possible for their kids. Which is why TFA sponsored a trip for a dozen or so community leaders and parents in January 2014 to visit some high-performing charter schools in Denver. "If you haven't had the experience of seeing a school that takes low-income kids actually outperforming white kids in suburbs," then you don't realize the possibilities for your own children.

There was "a lot of emotion" on the trip, says Curran – "a lot of tears, a lot of frustration." "If this could happen for first- or second-generation Latino kids in Denver, why can't it happen for kids within the bounds of a sovereign nation?"

Dan Nelson was one of the people invited to Denver. A facilities manager at one of the schools on Pine Ridge, Dan has a lot of interest in education. His sister works in a Montessori program. His son runs a Head Start program on the reservation, and his daughter teaches Lakota language at a local school. "The system that we have been using is tired. The teachers are helpless to control their work environments. They just do what they have to rather than being active in changing things. It's just that we are in need of a change."

Nelson actually spent part of his childhood in Denver and was amazed at how much things had changed. When he was growing up, a desegregation plan was put in place and kids were bused to different neighborhoods. "One thing that surprised me in Denver now is the freedom, the choice of schools they have." As a child, he experienced "a turbulent time." But on his trip, he saw "peacefulness and calm of it, the kids getting to go to whatever school they wanted to."

At the charter schools he visited, including a KIPP (Knowledge Is Power Program) academy, he says, "the kids have a light in their eyes. That's what impressed me." The kids at Pine Ridge, he says, might have that light too, but "it's dulled by our schools." There are plenty of "factions" on the reservation that are opposed to change, particularly people who work for the tribal government and the school system, according to Nelson. But "the only way for us to succeed is to start from scratch and build the school system the way we want it."

South Dakota is one of three states that don't allow charter schools. If the Indians of South Dakota were to support a charter law, it would probably pass. Nelson says he's not sure that charters are the solution, but "how do we know unless we get the opportunity? Why don't we have the freedom to choose where we send our kids?" Nelson is a father and a grandfather, and he tells me that he's speaking in that capacity, not as a professional in the school system.

He realizes that what he's saying is pretty radical on the reservation. And he's committed to spreading the message about the schools he saw. "All I can tell them is it's beautiful. It works. The best thing people can do is witness it for themselves. I want to take everyone there for five hours." The question is how many planeloads of people would he need to take there before the parents of Pine Ridge really started a revolution?

People like Nelson who want to see reform are up against some serious opposition from their own leadership. "We don't discuss charter schools," Fire Thunder tells me pointedly. "We have local control. We have school boards." She tells me that the tribe doesn't need a different structure for schools or the education system. "What we need is money to be creative to do what we need to do. The concepts are already here."

As for whether it might be useful to separate the running of schools from the school boards, Fire Thunder insists, "We keep politics separate from school operations. We are sophisticated enough not to let politics interfere."

Whatever Stacy Phelps thinks about Teach for America, he knows that's not true. In both his current role at the American Indian Institute for Innovation and his previous roles – including starting a math and science summer program for Native kids in Rapid City called GEAR UP – he realizes that the farther you can get from reservation politics, the better off you are. "God bless Cecilia [Fire Thunder]. She's working hard. She has all the major connections. [But s]he's not an educator."

When I bring up Fire Thunder's idea of the tribe developing its own academic standards, Phelps says he doesn't oppose that measure, but he notes, "We have the same obligation as white educators to get our kids reading at a proficient level." Phelps says that he and his colleagues "want the kids to be successful. We know they've got to leave their reservation. We don't have a successful tribal college. They've got to come off the reservation to go to a university." He doesn't want to understate the importance of Indian identity, but he does say that "being a Lakota means we have to walk in two different worlds."

Indeed, Stacy Phelps and his colleague Walt Swan tell me that they see the state standards for educating children as the "minimum." "What you put on top of that is the genuine mark, and that is our language and our culture." All of those things together "will make us better citizens, and that will give us more identity to be proud of who we are."

But the bureaucracy and the politics involved in Indian education – whether the schools are run by the tribe, the Bureau of Indian Affairs, or the state of South Dakota – seem insurmountable at times. How Indians can build a strong academic program with a strong cultural identity remains to be seen.

At Red Cloud, the boarding program officially ended in 1980, and the school has transformed its former dorms into housing for teachers and a Heritage Center. Red Cloud actually consists of three schools – two elementary schools and a high school. The facilities aren't posh by any stretch of the imagination, but some of the older buildings have a distinguished look, and the newer parts of campus are sleek and filled with light. There's an art gallery with paintings, sculptures, and artifacts of the local culture. And the school has launched the most extensive program anywhere to teach the Lakota language to children. Staff members work with nearby universities to preserve the language in both its written and its oral form.

Red Cloud is undertaking the most advanced educational experiments in Pine Ridge, and there seems to be universal agreement that

Red Cloud High School is the best on the reservation. Over 95 percent of its graduates go on to pursue higher education or postsecondary training.[18] Its graduates score about average for the state of South Dakota, which is hardly a high standard, but it's much better than for Indian students generally. Red Cloud has a significant advantage, though, which its critics are quick to point out: students are required to pass an entrance exam. (Interestingly, one elementary school I visited measures its progress over time by how many of its students pass the Red Cloud exam each year.)

But even given this standard, Clay Leonard, who has taught math at Red Cloud for 27 years, tells me that many incoming freshmen perform at a sixth- or seventh-grade level. "It is tough on the teachers, but the skill level is not up there, so your goal is to catch them up the best you can."

Some of Red Cloud's students have achieved tremendous success. In 1989, the Gates Millennium Scholarship, which covers the whole cost of college education, was awarded to a Red Cloud student. Today, a higher percentage of Red Cloud students have received the Gates Millennium Scholarship than at any other school in the country.[19] In part, at least, the teachers and administrators attribute this success to the school's religious identity. Which isn't to say it pushes the Catholic faith on its students. Most of the students identify as Christian, but relatively few of them are practicing Catholics. And Leonard believes there's very little tension over the fact that Red Cloud is a Catholic school. "The culture of the Lakota is so extensively integrated into our program. It's not that we want you to be Catholic. It's like we want you to improve your spirituality, and everybody has that." Using its Lakota and Catholic values, the school tries to provide students with a safe place – away from the chaos of their families and communities – as well as a sense of purpose and direction for their lives.

In the 1980s, the campus church was destroyed in a fire. The new Church of the Holy Rosary is a modern affair with lots of light streaming in, but the most interesting parts of it involve the melding of Lakota and Catholic tradition. The shape of a medicine wheel was incorporated into the design, and if you look closely at the Stations of the Cross around the chapel, you'll see that it's the U.S. cavalry rather than the Romans who are pursuing Jesus.

No one pays more than $100 a semester to attend Red Cloud. The school is funded almost entirely by donations from individuals and foundations. It runs a massive direct-mail campaign every year. People across the country send small donations. Some donate because it's a Catholic school. Some donate because they want to help Indians. Robert Brave Heart, who became the school's first lay Lakota superintendent in 2003, tells me that they run about 17 or 18 campaigns a year, and a lot of the checks that come in are for only $25. But sometimes they get lucky and someone leaves the school a more significant amount in a will or estate: "There was one for a million dollars that really put us in a good position a few years ago." Brave Heart notes that the appeals to donors used to be more about the terrible conditions on the reservations, but now they try to focus more on Red Cloud's educational successes.

"We can't pity the children. We can't feel sorry for them. We need to offer them opportunity for hope to be able to build a better life for themselves."

Despite Red Cloud's successes, the school has continued to incur the ire of many local residents. Aside from its boarding-school history, Brave Heart says the school had another break with the community in the early 2000s. It used to be run in consultation with a school board made up of some Jesuits and Franciscan nuns as well as some local laypeople. Brave Heart says that "it started to become political," so the administration decided to dissolve the board. That didn't go over well in the community.

A few years ago, as Fire Thunder tells me, the tribal council passed a law that would require that 2 percent of teachers' salaries go toward sustaining the tribal education department. Red Cloud hasn't paid, and Fire Thunder accuses school administrators of not respecting tribal laws. "They have excluded themselves. Red Cloud is not accountable to the tribe." Ultimately, despite the fact that Red Cloud is run by

Lakotas, despite the fact that it's helping Lakota students gain high-school diplomas and in some cases go on to great success in higher education, and despite the fact that it's preserving Lakota history through its heritage center and language program to an extent that no one else on the reservation is, many in tribal leadership still consider the school a pariah.

Ultimately, Keith Moore says, what's killing Indian education is politics. Whether it's Teach for America or charter schools, he notes that if tribal education directors see outsiders gaining too much influence, "they pull on the reins." Policies are changed at the drop of a hat. In fact, many people don't want to become school administrators on the reservation because if you make "one decision" people disagree with, you're "on the chopping block."

Moore is not despondent, however. One reason he left Washington was that he felt as if he wasn't making much of a difference there. But back home in South Dakota, he's still helping with GEAR UP, the math and science summer academy he started with Stacy Phelps a few years ago. Housed at the South Dakota School of Mines and Technology (in Rapid City), GEAR UP has helped prepare thousands of students for postsecondary education. Every alumnus of the program has graduated from high school, 87 percent have gone on to postsecondary education, and 9 percent have entered the military. Two-thirds of those who completed the program have graduated from college or are still enrolled.

Despite all the politics in Washington, in South Dakota, and especially on the reservation, Moore is hopeful about GEAR UP, about Teach for America, about the potential for charter schools, and about Red Cloud's success. In the fall of 2015, though, it was revealed that the company managing GEAR UP, the Mid-Central Educational Cooperative, had been under financial scrutiny by the Department of Education. State officials revoked its contract, and a criminal investigation was launched when the group's business manager killed his wife and four children before shooting himself and setting fire to their home.

Moore is unsure of what the future holds for reforming Indian education. "Do people have the tools to understand the necessity of a quality education system?" he asks me. And then he offers the real question that's eating at him: "How much longer can we educate students this poorly and make it as a people?"

PART THREE

Who Will Stand Up for Civil Rights?

CHAPTER FIVE

Equal Protection

The Tribe vs. the Individual

IN THE EARLY 1990S, Elizabeth Morris remembers reading about a case in which a 5-year-old boy who had been adopted as a baby was removed from his home by an Indian tribe in South Dakota. Morris and her late husband, Roland, who was a member of the Minnesota Chippewa Nation, were horrified to realize that if anything ever happened to them, their young children could be taken by her husband's tribe and raised on a reservation – all because of something called the Indian Child Welfare Act. As Morris told me: "His reservation is a dangerous place. It's not safe for children. He made a decision as a U.S. citizen not to raise his children there." The idea that a federal law could undermine that decision gives Morris nightmares, and she has made it her life's work to change it.

Her dealings with her husband's extended family and other people on the reservation have been difficult, to say the least. Morris has attended the funeral of a 2-year-old beaten to death there. She has fought off a drunken man trying to sexually assault a 10-year-old. She has raised four Indian foster children with fetal alcohol syndrome and two more born with crack in their bloodstream. Now she runs the Christian Alliance for Indian Child Welfare. Morris knows enough about the problems on some reservations to know that for too many children the best option is to be raised somewhere else.

But according to the provisions of ICWA, passed in 1978, tribal governments have a say over where children with the slightest trace of Indian blood are placed if there's ever a dispute over custody. In practice, this has meant that if parents voluntarily put such a child up for adoption, tribal governments can block that child's placement with a non-Indian family. Even if that child has never set foot on a reservation. Even if the biological mother thinks a non-Indian family might provide a better home. Even if the Indian family has no particular connection to Indian culture or heritage. And even if a non-Indian family off the reservation promises that they *will* expose the child to Indian culture.

Just as Morris and her husband were at one time, most Americans are largely unaware of ICWA. The law did gain a higher profile in 2013 with the Supreme Court ruling in *Adoptive Couple v. Baby Girl*,[1] which became known as the "Baby Veronica" case. The details of the case were so heartbreaking they became the stuff of television specials.

In 2009, a child was born to a Hispanic mother and a father who was an enrolled member of the Cherokee Nation. The two were engaged to be married, but she broke it off and gave him the option of paying child support or relinquishing his parental rights. He chose the latter. She put the child up for adoption through a private agency; a couple in South Carolina adopted the baby. Although the Cherokee Nation was supposed to be informed about the adoption, the father's name was misspelled in the paperwork, so the Cherokees didn't think he was a member. After learning that the mother had given up the child, the father had second thoughts about his decision and tried to get custody. If he hadn't been Indian, he wouldn't have had a legal leg to stand on. But because of his race, he could invoke ICWA.

The case worked its way up to the South Carolina Supreme Court, which ruled 3–2 in favor of the father. (If the paperwork had been done correctly, the child would have been with him the whole time.

There would've been no question about ICWA's relevance.) As a result, the child was removed from the home where she had lived with her adoptive parents from birth to age two and a half and sent to Oklahoma to live with people she had never met. The adoptive parents appealed to the U.S. Supreme Court, which reversed the lower court's decision and determined that the Indian Child Welfare Act didn't apply in cases where the biological parents had never been the child's custodial parents.

But the court seems to have left open some important questions. Such as why taking race into account in adoption cases is illegal for every group in the United States except Native Americans. And why is anyone determining custody of a child based on anything other than the best interests of that child? Why does a tribe's quest to ensure its demographic and cultural future matter when the welfare of a minor is at stake? And perhaps most importantly, are American Indian children really receiving equal protection under the law?

In his concurring opinion, Justice Clarence Thomas hinted at these problems. "The notion that Congress can direct state courts to apply different rules of evidence and procedure merely because a person of Indian descent is involved raises absurd possibilities. Such plenary power would allow Congress to dictate specific rules of criminal procedure for state-court prosecutions against Indian defendants. Likewise it would allow Congress to substitute federal law for state law when contract disputes involve Indians."[2]

Aside from its obviously discriminatory implications, Walter Olson, a senior fellow at the Cato Institute's Center for Constitutional Studies, says that "the not-very-well-disguised secret of ICWA is that it heavily benefits tribes, and the interests of individuals and families will be sacrificed to tribal interests." The initial victory that the biological father received in the Baby Veronica case, Olson says, "had nothing to do with the biological father. It had to do with the tribe. The tribe's rights trumped the child's rights."

In 2000, Johnston Moore and his wife took two foster kids, boys ages 4 and 5, into their home in Long Beach, California. They were told that one boy was Caucasian and one was Caucasian and Hispanic. The boys adjusted well; they even called Moore and his wife "Dad" and "Mom." Moore says, "It was a match made in heaven." He and his wife wanted to make the situation permanent.

One day they received a call from child services telling them that the boys' Indian paternal grandmother wanted custody. The court battle lasted years, despite the fact that the boys' biological mother favored the Moores. In any other case, a noncustodial grandparent would hardly be able to contest a legitimate adoption. But in order to hold on to their children, Moore and his wife had to convince the court that they were going to make them aware of their racial heritage. ICWA's provisions still outrage him. "A kid who is $1/512$th Cherokee and lives in Tallahassee? You're going to ask a tribe about him? Why should a tribe in Kansas get to determine where my kids are?"

Ultimately, Moore and his wife prevailed, but like so many others who have been exposed to the problems of ICWA, Moore is determined to change it.

"I don't believe that when a child needs foster care we need to take them off the reservation," he tells me. "If there are families there, great." He compares the situation to foreign adoptions. "It's the same as Chinese orphanages. If Chinese families would adopt them, great. Same with Kenya and Ukraine." But that doesn't happen in many Indian communities.

Moore founded the Coalition for the Protection of Indian Children and Families, a group devoted to reforming ICWA. He acknowledges that politicians had a "valid point" when the law was passed. "Social workers were coming in and applying non-Native standards and taking kids away from their families. Our government had this 'civilize the savage' mentality. There were organizations just trying to get kids off the reservations."

Like many federal laws related to Native Americans today, ICWA was passed with good intentions – to rectify the problem of too many Indian children being removed from their families and communities without good reason. As the Supreme Court noted in its 1989 decision on the constitutionality of ICWA, Congress found that "an alarmingly high percentage of Indian families [were being] broken up by the removal, often unwarranted, of the children from them by nontribal public and private agencies."

Sometimes social workers would cite poverty as a reason to remove a child from his or her family. Which is to say, they might determine that a child being raised in a loving family would be better off elsewhere – even if there was no suggestion that the child was in any real danger. (These standards, of course, would be enough to remove plenty of white children from their homes as well.) ICWA was enacted to stop what the Supreme Court called the "wholesale removal of Indian children from their homes" that resulted from such practices.

When Mark Fiddler, a member of the Turtle Mountain band of Chippewa Indians, graduated from the University of Minnesota Law School in 1988 and went to work as a public defender, the motivation behind ICWA really appealed to him. "I supported the idea of trying to keep Indian kids in Indian homes whenever possible. I tried to prevent their unwarranted removal." His office oversaw around 2,000 placements of Indian children each year. Later, when he went into private practice in Minnesota, he continued to represent Indian parents and kids.

Fiddler didn't grow up on a reservation, but he spent many of his childhood summers on a reservation with his uncle, in a home with no running water. But lack of indoor plumbing, in and of itself, didn't make his uncle an unfit parent, notes Fiddler. As public defenders, Fiddler says, "We were there to ferret out the removals based on prejudice. I subscribed to the theory that was the problem." The reason that so many children were being removed from their families, Fiddler assumed, was racism.

Over the years, Fiddler came to see there was another, much more significant, problem. "As I started handling more child protection cases and seeing up front the alcoholism and drug abuse history and the history of adults being sexually abused themselves and raped, then you realize this has been going on for generations." In other words, many of the children were being removed because they were in danger. And a disproportionately high number of Indian children are in danger every day.

If you compare Indian communities to other impoverished areas in the United States, you'll see similarities in terms of single motherhood, teen pregnancy, drug use, and violence. Indeed, Morris believes the core of the problem is "family disintegration," caused largely, she says, by government subsidies. Her husband was married once before, and he acknowledges that he wasn't always there for his wife and children. But, says Morris, "It didn't matter if he took off for three months on a binge. They had HUD housing, they had food stamps, fuel assistance, tribal health care. He wasn't needed. If he thought his family wouldn't have had food, he would have behaved differently. A man does need to feel needed. But the government took care of all that."

The government's replacement of the father in the home has devastated communities across the country, and not just Native American ones. But fatherlessness or unemployment alone can't explain the levels of child abuse and sexual abuse in Indian communities.

Most tribal leaders, health professionals, and observers of Indian communities blame boarding schools for the high rates of physical and sexual abuse on reservations. It's hard to determine exactly how many children went to boarding school willingly – many families, including Fiddler's, thought it was the best way to get an education – and how many were forcibly removed from their homes, but there's no doubt that there was widespread physical, sexual, and emotional abuse at these institutions. Children were ripped from their families and communities, they were forbidden from speaking their native language, and many were preyed upon by teachers and administrators. When they returned to their families, they often had difficulty functioning. Many adults still can't talk about their experiences. And it has significantly affected their ability to raise their own families.

Writing in the *New York Times*, Joe Flood, a high-school teacher on the Pine Ridge reservation, explains the epidemic of suicide there:

Tribal leaders and experts are struggling to understand the recent suicide epidemic (specifics on many of the cases aren't widely known), but there's general agreement on one underlying cause: the legacy of federally funded boarding schools that forcibly removed generations of Native American children from their homes. Former students and scholars of the institutions say that the isolation and lack of oversight at the mostly church-run schools allowed physical and sexual abuse to run rampant.[3]

Some media outlets seem to find it impossible to report about any social problem on an Indian reservation without mentioning these institutions. A recent NPR story on high levels of heroin abuse on reservations blamed boarding schools first. Once boarding schools were established as the primary reason for the problem, the reporter got around to explaining that "Mexican drug cartels are specifically targeting Indian Country. High unemployment on the reservations means many turn to trafficking and dealing. The cartels know the tribes lack law enforcement resources."[4] That seems to be a bit more of a direct connection than the idea that people are depressed and more likely to use drugs because they or their parents or grandparents attended a boarding school 25 or 50 years ago.

Still, regardless of whether the boarding-school experience can explain all the pathologies of Indian country, the schools have left an undeniable legacy. A mental health professional who has worked with residents of reservations tells the story of an enrolled member of a tribe in Montana who told him he used to poop in his pants rather than go to the bathroom so he wouldn't be sodomized by a priest at his boarding school. When the victim grew big enough to defend himself, the abuse finally stopped. But the victim also acknowledged that he turned around and did the same thing to younger children.

If you talk to residents of reservations, says Fiddler, "you realize this has been going on for generations." On the "macro-level," he notes, "you have this narrative about disproportionate placement rates" – that is, the idea that Indian children are being removed from their homes at a higher rate than children of other races. But then, says Fiddler, "there is the micro-level of reality with parents." He says that there's a "cycle of dysfunctional parenting that is passed from generation to generation."

One of the communities most devastated by this cycle has been the Spirit Lake reservation in North Dakota. The *New York Times* began one damning report on the reservation in 2012 as follows:

> The man who plays Santa Claus here is a registered child sex offender and a convicted rapist. One of the brothers of the tribal chairman raped a child, and a second brother sexually abused a 12-year-old girl. They are among a number of men convicted of sex crimes against children on this remote home of the Spirit Lake Sioux tribe, which has among the highest proportion of sex offenders in the country....
>
> The reservation has 38 registered sex offenders among its 6,200 residents, a rate of one offender for every 163 residents. By contrast, Grand Forks, N.D., about 85 miles away, has 13 sex offenders out of a population of 53,000 – a rate of about one in 4,000. In one home on the reservation, nine children are under the care of the father, an uncle and a grandfather, each a convicted sex offender, a federal official said. Two of the children, brothers who are 6 and 8, were recently observed engaging in public sex, residents said.[5]

The complete breakdown of civilization at Spirit Lake is a complicated story, and the blame lies partly with the tribal and federal officials who have let it go on. But let's stipulate that this behavior is not normal. Grown men don't generally prey on 12-year-olds. Young children don't engage in public sex. And poverty isn't enough to explain this depravity. There's something very disturbing happening in some of these communities.

And it's not only Spirit Lake. At the Red Lake Chippewa reservation in Minnesota, one mental health professional received reports of 75 children between the ages of 5 and 15 who were "dryhumping" and having sexual relations with each other on a school playground. Where did they learn this behavior?

For many reservation residents, there's little in the way of help for past abuses or any kind of rehabilitation. Joni Renbarger, who has worked as a psychologist for the Shoshone tribe as well as for Indian Health Services, tells me, "There are hardly any resources for these kids." There is "a lot of depression and anxiety" resulting from abuse. Renbarger has worked in different drug and alcohol treatment programs and been "shocked" by how badly run some of them are. "The files didn't even have labels on them with names. There was paperwork everywhere. They didn't even have a voicemail system or a file system."

The schools, she says, were of little help in handling the problems of these children. And Morris concurs that often the educational institutions were only contributing to the problems. Both on and off reservations, schools seem reluctant to crack down on poor performance and bad behavior from Indian kids.

Increasingly, Morris feels as if she's fighting a losing battle. The institutions that are supposed to be helping these children – from schools to the tribal health services to law enforcement – seem to be falling down on the job.

Renbarger typically sees clients on an outpatient basis, but she perceives tremendous need for an inpatient facility based on the severity of the addiction problems on the reservation. In addition to adults, she has worked with teenagers. "There is no family support. The parents are in jail or have already died. Or the parents are too busy with their own substance abuse. Some are living with grandparents."

Renbarger says that the "psychological and social problems of the community begin with child protection. The kids are shifted from family to family. There is neglect, abuse, and death. The situation perpetuates itself." She tells me that "the lack of stable environments for children" is the first problem that has to be tackled. Of course, there's "historical trauma," she acknowledges. "But the question is how do we move beyond that? Some of that has got to be providing secure, safe attachments for children who are being yanked around."

How can we put a stop to the cycle? The answer doesn't lie in simply improving the economic situation or educational outcomes. It has to involve better child services and better law enforcement. The people responsible for crimes against children need to be punished. Even if they're acting out because of some past trauma, they can't be permitted to inflict it on another generation. But there's a serious law enforcement problem here.

In 2012, Michael R. Tilus, director of behavioral health at the Spirit Lake Health Center, e-mailed state and federal health officials about what he saw as the "epidemic" of abuse on the reservation. In July of that year, according to a report in the *New York Times*, "a 2-month-old girl died there after tribal officials had received warnings of child abuse, according to a federal official, and in May 2011, a 9-year-old girl and her 6-year-old brother were sexually assaulted before being stabbed to death and left under a mattress. Their bloody bodies were discovered several days later."[6]

Tilus, who had worked for the Public Health Service for 10 years, was actually reprimanded for sending the e-mail. His superiors at the clinic at Spirit Lake accused him of "engaging in action and behavior of a dishonorable nature" because he hadn't gone through the proper channels to register his complaint. They rescinded his promotion and transferred him to another position.

Tilus responded to the punishment: "After significant thought and with great concern for the protection of my patients, I acted as a whistle-blower and made a lawful disclosure by raising my concerns about the health and safety of these abused children to more than just my direct supervisors, but to multiple appropriate agencies who could be intimately involved in resolving this public health crisis."[7]

A few days after the *Times* reported on the reprimand, the director of the Indian Health Service rescinded Tilus's punishment,[8] and in October 2012, the Bureau of Indian Affairs took over the tribe's social services. But according to an investigation by PBS's *Frontline*, "Some residents have questioned how much has changed." In February 2013, the Bureau of Indian Affairs conducted a "town-hall meeting," in which it told local congressmen as well as residents that it was "following up on several hundred abuse allegations and had hired additional staff to handle the high caseload."[9]

Meanwhile Thomas Sullivan, who was named regional administrator of the Administration for Children and Families in 2002, picked up where Tilus left off. So far he has issued 13 different "mandated reports" about the problems on Spirit Lake. They're mandated not because his superiors asked him for his input – they don't seem to want them. Rather, the reports are mandated by law, because teachers, psychologists, and others who work with vulnerable populations are required by law to report abuses. Here's a sample from Sullivan's most recent report:

> *The Tribal Elder who observed two little boys engaging in anal sex in her yard did call police immediately. No one in law enforcement took her statement. She tried to tell her story at the February 27, 2013 Hearing but she was shushed by the US Attorney, the BIA leadership and all of those on the platform. The US Attorney did say publicly that he would speak to her privately after the Hearing concluded. He did not. Nor did anyone from his office take her statement. How did these actions protect children?*
>
> *One day later, on February 28, 2013, these same two boys were observed by two little girls engaging in oral sex on a Spirit Lake school bus. The little girls reported this to the bus driver, their teachers and the school principal.*

> All of these responsible people kept quiet about this incident. None
> filed a Form 960 as required. How do these actions protect children?
> On March 14, 2013 law enforcement went to the home of these
> two boys because one of them tried to sexually assault a three year
> old female neighbor who is developmentally delayed.
> Police were called last summer when adults and very young chil-
> dren observed a 15 year old boy having intercourse with a 10 year old
> girl on the steps of the church in St. Michaels at mid-day. No one
> responded to the call.[10]

Sullivan's reports go on like this at length, each more exasperated than the last. He details incidents that have been reported to him by one or more reputable sources – including tribal leaders, law enforcement, and even a nun. He notes that either no action has been taken or someone has provided some absurd excuse – people have told him that sex between a man and an adolescent girl hadn't been further investigated because it was "consensual." His sources have been threatened. Sullivan has been barred by his superiors from speaking with the media. But he continues, in the face of what is clearly a threat to his career and quite possibly his physical safety, to document the horrors at Spirit Lake.

In one of his reports, he compares the situation at Spirit Lake to the situation at Penn State or in the Catholic Church. The authorities knew about the problems and looked the other way. Now the problems have been publicized, and people continue to look the other way.

Perhaps a better comparison is to the case of Rotherham, England, where widespread child abuse was found to have taken place between 1997 and 2013. Investigators uncovered almost 1,400 cases of abuse, many of which had been documented in reports by a Home Office researcher in 2002.[11] When the news broke, many people wondered how these horrors could have been ignored for so long. The reports were suppressed out of "political correctness," some in British government have speculated, because the perpetrators and the local political leadership were largely of Muslim descent.[12]

Denis MacShane, Rotherham's former representative in Parliament, told the BBC that he should have done more to find out the truth of what was going on. He admitted he should have "burrowed into" the issue: "I think there was a culture of not wanting to rock the multicultural community boat if I may put it like that." He said that his liberal views made him reluctant to raise the issue of how the Muslim community treated women.[13]

Just as British leaders didn't want to accuse a largely Muslim community of abusing young girls, so the U.S. government doesn't want to make too much of an Indian community engaging in widespread child abuse. There's so much guilt about racism, about what was done to these communities in the past, that they don't want to shine a light on crimes taking place now. But the truth is that, in the name of protecting these communities, we're failing to protect their most vulnerable members.

Mark Fiddler used to believe that the most important thing for a child was to have "culturally appropriate" parenting: Indian children should be raised by Indian parents. But he says there was a "sea change" in his thinking in the mid-'90s as he started to learn about "attachment theory." According to a report by the U.S. Department of Health and Human Services, "The importance of early infant attachment cannot be overstated." The research has been clear for some time that children raised in stable environments with attentive parents have better outcomes in life. As the report concludes: "Children with secure attachments have more basic trust than those who are anxiously attached. They have more ego resiliency through early and middle childhood, unless they experience significant negative changes. They can also cope with setbacks, and recover more quickly. Securely attached children have more flexibility in processing current information and in responding appropriately in new situations and relationships."[14]

"What a child needs growing up is stability and permanent relationships irrespective of culture," says Fiddler. In fact, he adds, "Healthy attachment is a predicate for cultural knowledge." In all his litigation, he says, "my impetus is about the child's attachments and protecting the child's best interests. The theory behind ICWA is that Indian children won't be screwed up as long as they're parented by Indians. But the scientific evidence points to the fact that attachment is not related to the race of the caregiver."

In fact, what's destroying Indian communities isn't simply a "cycle of dysfunctional parenting." A shocking number of children also have had exposure to alcohol in utero. Fetal alcohol syndrome can have severe effects on a child's ability to learn, ability to judge consequences of his or her actions, and impulse control.

Jody Allen Crowe, a former teacher and principal who has served on six different reservations, has witnessed the effects of fetal alcohol syndrome firsthand. In his book *Fatal Link*, Crow describes his first years teaching: "So many students were unable to read and write. More had behavioral difficulties.... Some were violent. Many were promiscuous. Suicides were prevalent. Some were predators, others were very vulnerable." As evidenced by the fact that many of his students would soil themselves and then not be embarrassed about it, he says that a "majority of my students [were] having a difficult time, with few functioning at or possibly near their chronological age."[15]

Now the founder of Healthy Brains for Children, a nonprofit devoted to lowering the incidence of prenatal exposure to alcohol, Crowe describes his own ignorance at the time. "The impact of brain damage from alcohol was evident in their social behaviors, [in] their academic behaviors and in their physical characteristics, but I did not have a clue that what I was seeing was evidence of prenatal exposure to alcohol."[16]

According to a report by the U.S. Department of Health and Human Services, "Native Americans have some of the highest rates of fetal alcohol syndrome in the nation. Among some tribes, the rates are as high as 1.5 to 2.5 per 1,000 live births. Among others, the rates are comparable to that of the general population in the United States and range between 0.2 to 1.0."[17] If anything, children with fetal alcohol syndrome need even more resources and parental supervision than typical children. But child services on reservations are often overburdened, and sometimes they're downright corrupt and incompetent. And ICWA is helping ensure that the list of adults who can take these children in is shorter, not longer.

For some children, there are simply no responsible adults in the picture. And on a few reservations, adults are simply covering up the problems. Renbarger sits on a child protection team with officials from the FBI, the Bureau of Indian Affairs, and caseworkers for the tribe. "There is a shortage of homes" to put these kids in, she notes. "And there are no background checks before placing someone in foster care. There are sexual abusers who have access to these kids."

Elizabeth Morris confirms this from personal experience. For 17 years, Morris and her husband served as foster parents. When they first applied to be foster parents, "two social workers showed up at our house for an hour or two. They walked through the house. They didn't look at the bedrooms. They didn't care. After that, they asked us how to get to the National Bison Range. They were supposed to be observing us for two days, but they spent the rest of the time sightseeing. We could have been ax murderers." And once a family is approved as an "ICWA" family – that is, cleared to take in Indian children – Morris says, "There is no follow-up."

Part of the problem, Renbarger notes, is manpower. In her case, she says, "There are a handful of agents working with a community of 20,000 people. If there's a murder that happens that week, they have to go out and work that. Some of these child abuse cases get overlooked." Meanwhile, she says, the tribal department of social services is supposed to be on call at all times to deal with these issues. But she has found herself "frustrated in trying to get a hold of them." There have been instances where "they told the FBI agent to place the kid. That's the attitude. They're so overwhelmed themselves, but they don't have competent leadership or direction either."

She says the "tribal departments of social services are incompetent, and there is not good oversight from the state level or from the Bureau of Indian Affairs." Indeed, court orders for child protection "are not drawn up in a timely manner." The court systems are often part of the problem. "They don't have the same standards as state courts." She gives the example that the judges are often related to the families whose cases they're deciding. For the children, "it's hard not to feel helpless in that kind of environment."

Although it would be helpful for the workers to have smaller case-loads, Renbarger says, "My gut tells me that more money being thrown isn't necessarily the answer. There has to be some fundamental paradigm shift."

Where to start? With some honesty, for one thing. The fact that his supervisors' apparent first impulse was to punish Tilus for speaking about these abuses tells us something about the system. The fact that Sullivan is barred from speaking to the media tells us something about the system. There's tremendous fear about even naming the problem, and there's a tendency to place the blame on others.

Take the 2013 reauthorization of the Violence Against Women Act. A provision in the bill expanded Indian tribal courts' powers to prosecute non-Indians accused of sexual assault on Indian lands. Title IX of VAWA authorizes "special domestic violence criminal jurisdiction."[18] Under this provision, tribes may criminally prosecute *non-Indians* for the crimes of domestic violence, dating violence, and the violation of protection orders.

Kimberly Norris Guerrero, an actress and tribal advocate who's Cherokee and Colville Indian, told the *Washington Post*: "Over the years, what happened is that white men, non-native men, would go onto a Native American reservation and go hunting – rape, abuse and even murder a native woman, and there's absolutely nothing anyone could do to them.... They got off scot-free."[19]

Rape and sexual abuse are clearly rampant on many Indian reservations. According to the Justice Department, one in three Native American women will be raped in her lifetime.[20] In a 2007 story on the Standing Rock Sioux reservation in the Dakotas, doctors told NPR that they saw rape and sexual assault victims "several times a month" but that they were almost never called to testify in court. And authorities rarely break out a rape kit when a woman reports a rape.[21]

In 86 percent of cases of sexual assault against Indians, the victims claim their attackers were non-Indians. That's a Justice Department statistic that also appeared in the *Washington Post*.[22] But despite numerous calls to the Justice Department and e-mails to the *Washington Post*, I haven't been able to get a copy of the report that yielded that number. And the Justice Department official to whom I spoke was unable to explain to me the methodology behind it either. He did say, "It's not a number we like to rely on." And he noted that he issued a similar warning to the *Washington Post* reporter.

Moreover, another Justice Department report makes that number seem suspect. According to the 2013 "Indian Country Investigations and Prosecutions" report, the vast majority of crimes, including sexual assaults, committed against Indians on reservations are perpetrated by *other Indians*. A table on the "Status of Victim and Subject in Indian Country Investigations"[23] that were "administratively closed that year" found 425 Indian subjects, compared to 32 non-Indian subjects. Among sexual assaults in particular, the numbers were 29 and 5. In other words, in about 85 percent of the FBI's sexual assault cases closed on Indian lands, the perpetrators were Indian.

Those numbers look to be similar in previous years. Although many reservation residents are non-Indian, and many reservations are adjacent to large cities with mixed populations, the idea that people of other races are coming to reservations to "hunt" Indian women seems questionable at best.

Even if Indians on reservations account for only a quarter of the total Indian population in the United States, it's pretty hard to imagine that there were enough assaults perpetrated by non-Indians against Indians on reservations to get to that 86 percent. And, if anything, one would think the cases taken and closed by the FBI would be more likely, not less likely, to involve racial incidents, where the question of jurisdiction across reservation boundaries and state boundaries might be more pronounced.

The claim that attacks on Indians are perpetrated mostly by non-Indians has been made before, though, including in a 2004 report from the Bureau of Justice Statistics. In 2008, South Dakota attorney general Larry Long and University of South Dakota researchers looked at the claim. Their subsequent article, "Understanding Contextual Differences in American Indian Criminal Justice," appeared in the *American Indian Culture and Research Journal*.[24]

They pointed to a number of flaws in the BJS data, including that it was based largely on a survey of victims rather than on actual crime data. Looking at state data, Long found that nearly 73 percent of Indian homicides were committed by other Indians. "From our analysis, we found that intentional homicide is predominantly intra-racial in South Dakota, contrary to the [Bureau of Justice Statistics] findings." As for rapes, they found that in South Dakota, 69 percent of Indian victims were assaulted by other Indians. "Contrary to the [Bureau of Justice Statistics'] national findings, rape is predominantly intra-racial in South Dakota," Long and his co-authors wrote.[25]

Trumpeting the new provisions of VAWA, Thomas J. Perrelli, a former associate attorney general, told the *Washington Post*: "There are tribal communities where state police have no jurisdiction and federal law enforcement has jurisdiction but is distant and often unable to respond.... There are tribal communities where the federal government has no jurisdiction but state law enforcement, which has jurisdiction, does not intervene. And there are still other tribal lands where there is a dispute about who, if anyone, has jurisdiction. All of this has led to an inadequate response to the plight of many Native American women."[26]

From my interviews, it seems clear that there has been an inadequate response on the part of law enforcement. And it also seems clear that there are problems with jurisdiction. When I recently asked a group of three Native American leaders to whom they would report a case of child abuse on their respective reservations, one said the tribal leaders, one said state officials, and one said the FBI.

But it seems doubtful that the solution to these problems is to give more power to tribal governments, who in many cases can't deal with the problems they already have.

Just like the Catholic Church and the Penn State administration, or, for that matter, the Satmar ultra-Orthodox Jewish community in Brooklyn, Indian reservations are insular. Sometimes the people deciding the cases are related to the defendants. Reservations are often governed by old boys' networks that can, if left unchecked, put tribal leaders' interests ahead of victims' interests, even in cases of sexual crime. We can't let the foxes guard the henhouse.

Then there's the problem of the tribal "justice" systems. These courts just don't offer the same kind of procedures and protections as the rest of our judicial system. And as Christina Villegas of the Independent Women's Forum tells me, "The problem with the tribal courts is that they don't necessarily adhere to the same constitutional standards as the other courts in this country."

Her point is backed by the National Association of Criminal Defense Lawyers. In a letter warning the House of Representatives against expanding tribal powers, the group notes that many tribes "do not make the code of laws publicly available" and "have no rules for discovery by the defendants of evidence against them." Indeed, many tribes don't even provide defendants with a lawyer to represent them at trial.[27]

In all cases, but especially in rape cases, the collection and discovery of evidence is extremely important. As Villegas notes, without evidence and a clear judicial process, the cases just "descend into 'he said, she said.'" Rather than giving over more power to Indian tribes, we should be giving women on these reservations greater access to the same courts (and police) that the rest of us get to use.

But there are other forces standing in the way as well. In April 2015, a federal panel was formed to find out whether Native Americans living on reservations "are subject to disproportionately harsher punishments for crimes than other Americans," according to an article in the *Wall Street Journal*. Because Indians on reservations are typically prosecuted under federal law and not state law, the punishments can be heavier.

The article notes, "In South Dakota, Native Americans make up nearly 60% of the federal caseload, but only 9% of the population." Such statistical comparisons are often used with other minority groups to suggest that there's a policing or a sentencing disparity. But there's a key figure missing from such analysis: what percentage of crimes are being committed by Indians in South Dakota? If Indians make up a disproportionate number of victims, and, as former attorney general Larry Long notes, most of these crimes are intra-racial, then we can presume that Indians are perpetrating a disproportionate amount of the crime.

But even if it's true that Indians are being sentenced more harshly because they're being sentenced in federal court, what's the alternative? Either give more power to prosecute to the tribes themselves – the effect of which will probably be less effective policing and prosecution. Or give power to the states – which the tribes would never go for because they want to maintain their sovereignty. Or change the sentencing guidelines in federal courts for Indians. All in all, this doesn't sound like a winning proposition.

None of these issues are new for William Allen, who served on the U.S. Commission on Civil Rights from 1987 to 1992. Allen describes the questions that came before the commission concerning Indians. "They were primarily law enforcement issues, the extent to which there were protections for people in the law enforcement environment." He became especially concerned "with the lack of coordination between the tribal police and the Bureau of Indian Affairs and the FBI and Justice Department." There seemed, according to Allen, "to be a pattern of deference to tribal authority that left them substantially unaccountable."

Beginning with the 1978 Supreme Court case of *Santa Clara Pueblo v. Martinez,*[28] Allen notes that the protections afforded Indians by the U.S. Constitution seemed to narrow while the definition of tribal sovereignty seemed to expand. In that case, a member of the Santa Clara Pueblo brought suit against her tribe because of a rule denying membership to children of women who married out of the tribe but not to children of men who did the same. The court held that the tribe was protected from such suits because the Indian Civil Rights Act of 1968 "does not expressly authorize the bringing of civil actions for declaratory or injunctive relief to enforce its substantive provisions." But for all intents and purposes it meant that tribes could discriminate based on gender, even if local, state, and federal government institutions were prohibited from doing so. There was a different set of rules in place for Indians.

Some cases Allen and his colleagues looked at involved people who were denied the right to counsel by a tribal court. In other cases there were "problems with conflicts of interest in the administration of justice." Others involved civil matters: "People engaged in a business enterprise on a reservation would receive no due process guarantees with regard to how their businesses might be treated or licensing criteria or even unpromulgated regulatory intrusions upon them."

Allen also notes that a new set of civil rights challenges came up with the advent of casinos on Indian land. "Tribal ownership of the casinos was achieved through a kind of cartelization process." Trying not to be "prejudicial," Allen notes, "they came to be greatly wound up with shadowy activity. There seemed to have been criminal beings that got involved in the business in association with the tribes, and it made tribal membership itself a commodity." Since the members of the tribe would be sharing in the wealth generated by the casinos, "people were deregistered against their will.... Other people discovered an Indian heritage they had previously forgotten."

From a political perspective, says Allen, there wasn't a lot of difference between Republicans and Democrats on these issues. The staff at the Commission on Civil Rights, he notes, were "close to the Justice

Department people, who were sympathetic to the tribal sovereignty argument and therefore sought to limit the thrust of the commission's investigations."

But over the course of the years he was on the commission, Allen says, "we began to receive testimony [about ICWA], an area we had not ourselves identified as a target of the inquiry." The cases were so "heartwrenching" that "eventually we had to give some attention to this."

Allen says he was "greatly affected" by the stories he heard because "they exemplified the suspension of the most ordinary forms of judicial prudence in the child care area." He says that U.S. courts have a "pretty elaborate system of looking after the best interests of the child." But here was "dramatic evidence that the laws were operating so as to exclude those standard protections for those of Indian descent." Because the discrepancy was affecting young children, he says, "it seemed even more damning in my eyes than many of the other abuses that we had uncovered."

Since leaving the commission, Allen has maintained an interest in the problems of the Indian Child Welfare Act. "A simple question had gone unasked in the course of developing and implementing [it], and that was 'What was the best interest of these children?'"

In Allen's view, state courts were left unable to deal with the cases because ICWA is a federal statute. And "children were caught in this shadowland where there is no essential protection." Although state courts can be quite aggressive in dealing with child welfare issues, "you do not have the same aggressive patented intervention on reservations, which means that the children are often left in circumstances of abuse from which, if they had not been on reservations, they would have been removed."

Allen is quick to acknowledge that not every reservation has the same abuse problems I have described here. "But there's enough of a problem that it's fair to say it's a broken system." And it's broken because of "the vacuum created by federal unwillingness to intrude upon the activities of tribes."

In Allen's view, there's really only one way to solve the persistent violation of individual rights on reservations. And that's to erect the reservations as states under the Constitution. For smaller tribes, this would probably not be feasible, Allen says, but for larger ones, it's the only answer. They would have the same kind of sovereignty that states have, and federal powers would be limited to those enumerated in the Constitution. But the residents of those reservations would finally be entitled to all the protections of citizens of the United States.

Unfortunately, the political climate both on and off reservations is such that it's unlikely any significant changes will occur soon. American Indians living on reservations who see the problems with law enforcement, child protection, and even the court system and who worry about the safety of themselves and their children do have an option – they can leave. And many of them do. People like Elizabeth Morris and her late husband saw that the reservation was no place for their children. Indeed, for decades, reservations were losing population as residents increasingly realized there were more opportunities elsewhere.

But once President Nixon signed the Indian Self-Determination and Education Assistance Act in 1975, things started to change. The law made it possible for the federal government to give tribes direct grants for programs in law enforcement, education, child care, and environmental protection. The dollars were tied to population numbers. As Allen notes, "After that, you began to get a steady stream of people coming back into the reservation, because it came with some pretty targeted federal funding."

Today it's the most vulnerable people who remain on the reservation. They're the ones with little education, little sense of what life outside of the reservation might offer them, or little ambition. The jumble of legal jurisdictions has made it all but impossible to adequately police some reservations. And older Indians report that the lawlessness has worsened in recent years.

In part out of a desire not to trample on the so-called sovereignty of Indian nations, we're not offering Indians on reservations the same protections due to all American citizens. No one has made them aware of their rights as American citizens, and they often have no idea how to pursue remedies in court. Meanwhile the politicians who represent these tribes have no incentive to change things. Tribal leaders only demand more money from Washington to fix their problems. And the senators and congressmen who represent them are only too glad to oblige in return for the votes of these populations.

So the question is who will stand up for the civil rights of individual Indians? Who will say that it's not simply the collective interests of the tribe or the personal interests of tribal leaders that matter?

A great many people seem to be falling down on this job. Law enforcement is often ineffective, and jurisdictional questions can thwart even its agents' best efforts. The court systems often can't guarantee the rights of victims or of defendants. And the federal government is reluctant to step into the middle of things. Not only is there a sense that tribes deserve "sovereignty" – whatever that has come to mean – there's an overwhelming sense that political correctness pervades our conversation about American Indians. How can we fault them for anything when we have mistreated them so egregiously in the past? How can we hold them accountable for their actions now?

"The idea of forgiveness is unheard of for some people," Renbarger tells me, which is unfortunate because "hanging on to the anger about the white man does no good, and it perpetuates a lot of the issues affecting Indians."

Indeed, if tribal leaders' attitudes and Washington's policies don't change soon, another generation of Indians will be lost to the epidemics of drugs, abuse, and suicide. If Americans owe something to Indians, it's surely the basic protections we afford all Americans.

Native Americans as Americans

IN JULY 2014, members of the Quechan Tribe, who live on the Fort Yuma Indian reservation in California and Arizona, refused to accept money from the foundation of Dan Snyder, the owner of the Washington Redskins.[1] The residents of Fort Yuma, who number only a couple thousand, are not well off. According to the 2010 census, the poverty rate on the reservation is 37 percent. Alcoholism and unemployment are rampant. And suicide among young men is a serious problem (indeed, suicide is the second most common cause of death for Indians under the age of 35 nationally). The tribe had been trying to raise $250,000 for a skate park as part of an effort to curb youth suicide. Which is where Dan Snyder came in.

His Original Americans Foundation, launched in 2014 at the height of the controversy over whether his team's name should be changed because it was offensive to Indians, has been funding small projects like the construction of playgrounds on reservations. If the foundation sees that leaders of a tribe need money for a project, it tries to respond. But the Quechans decided they weren't going to take what one observer called "hush money." "We will not align ourselves with an

organization to simply become a statistic in their fight for name accep-
tance in Native communities," said Kenrick Escalanti, who attended
the meetings. "We know bribe money when we see it."[2]

Regardless of where you come down on the question of the team's
name, it seems clear that Snyder was hoping to earn some points
among American Indians and among the public at large with these
projects, which also include donating coats and shoes to poor children
on reservations. And boy, did he need some good press. Not only were
Native groups petitioning Twitter, Google, and Facebook to remove
the accounts belonging to the Redskins,[3] but the president himself got
involved.

"I don't know whether our attachment to a particular name should
override the real legitimate concerns people have about these things,"[4]
President Obama told the Associated Press. But then the administration's lawyers took things a step further and went about stripping the
team of its trademark protections, thereby inflicting financial harm
on Snyder.

Things were spinning out of control for the Redskins. In a letter
introducing the foundation, Snyder wrote, "The mission of the Original Americans Foundation is to provide meaningful and measurable
resources that provide genuine opportunities for Tribal communities.... Our efforts will address the urgent challenges plaguing Indian
country based on what Tribal leaders tell us they need most. We may
have created this new organization, but the direction of the Foundation is truly theirs."[5]

The Quechans weren't buying it. "After explaining to them how
much the project was going to cost," Escalanti recalled, "the reps met
with me and said, 'Look, we want to take care of this park for you.' That
was the moment that I felt weird. If it was that easy for them, what
does it mean for us to take money from them?"[6]

Good question. Tribal leaders – both at Fort Yuma and elsewhere –
might want to ask themselves that sort of thing a little more often.
And they might want to ask it about other money as well – especially
money coming from the federal government. It has been relatively

easy for Washington, as it has for Snyder, to throw more money at Indian reservations. And like Snyder's, that money has done more to assuage the guilt of the givers than to solve any of the problems on reservations. And the truth of the matter is that whatever harm Dan Snyder has done to American Indians with his continued use of the name Redskins, the federal government – as we have seen throughout this book – has done much, much worse.

But to many, the issue is larger than money. The National Congress of American Indians demanded the Redskins' name be changed because "the self esteem of Native youth is harmfully impacted, their self confidence erodes, and their sense of identity is severely damaged ... [when exposed to] "Indian-based names, mascots, and logos in sports."[7]

Writing in the *Claremont Review of Books*, William Voegeli took issue with the NCAI's claim, noting that the NCAI "moves directly from these premises to discuss how Indians are disproportionately likely to be victims of suicide and hate crimes. It does not even attempt to establish a causal relationship between these dire outcomes and the psychological changes it deplores. What's more, its social scientific argument for a cause-and-effect relationship between Indian mascots and Native youth's impaired self-esteem rests on a single ten-page conference paper by an assistant professor of psychology."[8] And that paper seems to rest on an experiment performed on a group of 172 American Indian students at one university in the Midwest.

But again, let's assume that the study was correct – that mascots have some measurable effect on the way young Indians see themselves. We should ask ourselves this important question: compared to what? If you've grown up in poverty, living with a single parent or no parent, surrounded by adults who have problems with drugs and alcohol, and you have no educational options and not much hope of employment ahead of you, is the image of an Indian on a football team's jersey going to push you over the edge?

What's insulting is the idea that the horrific problems that Native American youth experience are the result of a few politically incorrect words. Tribal leaders who try to instill a tradition of bravery and resilience in their youth know better. And the rest of us should too.

But we don't. Each year, thousands of people gather across the country to protest Columbus Day, accusing the explorer of launching a genocide. Last year, Seattle's city council voted to change the name of the federal holiday to "Indigenous Peoples' Day."[9] Minneapolis did the same. South Dakota celebrates Native American Day instead. Columbus Day is one of the least celebrated federal holidays in America, according to the Pew Research Center.[10] No one wants to recognize a holiday that has come to be associated with such conflict and controversy.

Glenn Morris, a professor at the University of Colorado at Denver and someone whom the Grand Governing Council of the American Indian Movement identified as a "Caucasian American masquerading as an Indian,"[11] is one of those leading his state's protest against the holiday. He explains that Columbus Day is a "hegemonic tool.... And it exists in part to advance a national ideology of celebrating invasion, conquest and colonialism."[12]

Whether or not you agree, you might wonder just how Morris's campaign to do away with Columbus Day is going to help the average American Indian. The short answer is it won't.

Neither, for that matter, will the resolution passed in 2014 by the Catholic Leadership Conference of Women Religious asking the pope to repudiate the "Doctrine of Discovery." The nuns, led by Sister Maureen Fiedler, objected to the 15th-century doctrine that gave Christian explorers the right to claim any land not already inhabited by Christians. The letter to the pope says that if he rebukes the doctrine, "all will know that today's world is different from the 15th century as we move away from patterns of domination and dehumanization." Most people probably already know that. But Fiedler believes that she's speaking up on behalf of "Native Americans, who are so seldom heard."[13]

In 2014, *The Chronicle of Higher Education* ran an article demanding to know "Why So Few American Indian PhDs?"[14] The headline would be funny if it weren't so sad. Only 51 percent of American Indian students in the class of 2010 received a high-school diploma. That number was down from 54 percent in 2008.[15] The real question we should be asking is why are we talking about doctorates? But that hasn't stopped the Alfred P. Sloan Foundation from giving grants to colleges that award more Indians PhDs. At Purdue, the grant has been used to foster community among Indians, creating, according to the *Chronicle*, "an educational and cultural center where American Indian students can hang out."

Indeed, many well-meaning Native and non-Native leaders are convinced that what Indians need to succeed is to have their cultures celebrated, to have their voices heard, to have their wounds healed with political protest. But decades of righteous indignation have proved fruitless.

In a harrowing essay for *Books and Culture*, James Calvin Schaap, an emeritus English professor at Dordt College, tells the story of the Dakota War of 1862, a conflict between the U.S. Army and several bands of the Eastern Sioux. Treaty violations had caused hunger and deprivation among the Sioux, and they decided to attack the local settlers. No fewer than 800 were killed. Schaap says, "To this day, among white people, stories of horrifying mutilation may well be the most memorable aspect of the war's legacy, the only stories that can't be forgotten."[16]

And the retaliation by U.S. soldiers was also brutal, with the capture of more than 1,000 Sioux. Thirty-eight of them were hanged, in the largest mass execution in American history. Schaap, who lives in Sioux Center, Iowa, in the area where most of these horrors took place, wrote, "I've tried to live in the story as best I can from the distance of time and place. I've tried to tell it as fairly as I could.... But even as it echoes in my heart, I can't help wondering if, in fact, we would all be better off simply to forget."

Such a sentiment runs contrary to everything most people believe about the imperatives of understanding history, of honoring the memories of our ancestors and the ancestors of those we have sinned against. And Schaap himself can't turn away from the past. "I can feel in my bones the anger and resentment of the Dakota at scurrilous agents, empty promises, and a legacy of broken treaties. But I also know I could come to hate the red man for the murders of babies yet to be born, of children, of women and men. I can feel those emotional tremors in me, rising, rising. And with that realization, my soul weeps."[17]

For better or worse, some measure of forgetting may be necessary in order to end this painful chapter in American history. Yet the need for more cultural sensitivity imbues just about every policy suggestion when it comes to American Indians. Take, for example, a paper published in the *Annals of the New York Academy of Sciences* called "Poverty and Health Disparities for American Indian and Alaska Native Children." After going on at length about the social, economic, and health deficits suffered by Indian children, the authors suggest early childhood interventions. Not only do the authors emphasize the need for these programs to be run collaboratively with the tribes themselves, but "educational institutions must acknowledge that communities often identify norms for what is considered desirable behavior and goals of education.... Doing so means reconsidering the use and validity of traditional means of assessing behaviors and educational achievement." In other words, if we just stop holding Indian kids to the same measures of good behavior and academic achievement to which we hold white kids, they can succeed.[18]

But how then to determine success? If most reasonable people can agree that poverty, unemployment, family disintegration, alcoholism, suicide, and domestic abuse are problems for any community, not just predominantly white communities, then we have to apply some of the same standards for achievement and behavior that we know can help combat them. Kids who are cared for in responsible two-parent families will do better in school, and those who do well in school will be more likely to find jobs. Those adults will in turn be better able to take care of their own children. Perhaps this sounds like an overly simplistic formula. But the truth of the matter is that when it comes to racial minorities in this country we too often engage in what George W. Bush famously called "the soft bigotry of low expectations."

In 2013, Congress passed a resolution authorizing the National Museum of the American Indian to create a memorial on its grounds to honor Indian veterans. American Indians, it turns out, have served in the military at the highest rate of any group since the American Revolution. According to the Defense Department, as of 2012 there were more than 22,000 American Indians and Alaska Natives on active duty, and the 2010 census identified over 150,000 American Indian and Alaska Native veterans. Twenty-seven have been awarded the Medal of Honor.

Writing about the memorial in May 2015, Kevin Gover, director of the museum and a member of the Pawnee Nation of Oklahoma, explained the history:

> *I've witnessed first-hand why Native Americans feel compelled to serve. I was raised with stories of friends and family members' bravery on the battlefield. Native Americans served in World War I even though they were not citizens of the United States. In fact, it was not until after World War II in the 1965 passage of the Voting Rights Act that all states were required to allow Native Americans to vote on the same basis as any other American. Despite decades of persecution and broken promises, despite being dispossessed of, and often forcibly removed from, their ancestral homelands, American Indians have served and continue to serve in our nation's armed forces in numbers that belie their small percentage of the American population. They step forward when duty calls.*[19]

Indeed, despite centuries of broken promises from the federal government, despite the bitterness that often pervades Indian communities, and despite years of being told by their own leaders and by

Washington's that they must remain a people apart, American Indians largely see themselves as Americans.

For every religious, ethnic, and racial minority in America, identity is a complicated topic. Are you a Jewish American or an American Jew? Are you Hispanic or Puerto Rican? How much does the specific place your ancestors came from matter as opposed to the way you distinguish yourselves from others in this country? Is it important that you look like your brethren or just that you have similar ancestry? And how much does your family background affect your daily life?

For American Indians, the questions are similar. And the answers vary significantly from tribe to tribe, from community to community, and from family to family. The fact that a significant portion of the population continues to live apart does make their situation different. Assimilation for American Indians didn't happen as quickly or as quietly as it did with so many newcomers to this country. But you can't spend much time on a reservation today without realizing how much the young people especially have absorbed mainstream American culture. The music coming from their cars, the videos on their phones, the clothing they wear – these are largely the same as in any area of the country.

Nor is it just American popular culture that's pervasive on reservations. For the most part, American Indians want to be a part of this country, and they see the markers of their success in the same way that most other Americans do. They want their children to be well educated and have the opportunity to choose the best life path for themselves – to make enough money and pursue fulfilling jobs while retaining strong family and community ties and holding close the traditions of their ancestors.

Whereas some would prefer that children stay close to home, others see the necessity of pushing their children out in order to achieve what they want. Either way, they want to see their children grow up with a knowledge and understanding of Native traditions and Native languages.

But just as for any ethnic group in this country, keeping those traditions becomes more difficult with each passing year. When we think about American Indians in the context of other minority groups, it becomes clear that their cultural experience is not unique. For better or worse, they're experiencing the same kind of assimilation as other groups. Once the traditions and the language are no longer the default for the whole community, they require serious effort to maintain. The children of Korean immigrants may no longer speak Korean at home, but if parents want their children to know Korean, they can pay someone to teach it to them.

Not surprisingly, the Indian communities that have done the most to hold on to their language and cultural traditions have tended to be those with the most money – in other words, those that have most adapted themselves to the American economic system and way of life. Thanks to the revenues from the Foxwoods Casino in Connecticut, for instance, the Pequot Indians were able to open up a massive museum and research center dedicated to their heritage. Pine Ridge's Red Cloud Indian School, thanks to donations from outsiders, has been able to devote resources to the systematic study and teaching of the Lakota language. When communities are at a loss for food and housing, on the other hand, they simply can't spend much time worrying about recouping cultural losses.

Although many tribal leaders believe that the key to raising up their communities is reintroducing young people to their cultural and linguistic heritage, it's not enough to solve their problems, and it probably isn't the best first step either. As Keith Moore, former director of the Bureau of Indian Education, noted, it's only one piece of a hundred-piece educational puzzle.

The cultural problems on Indian reservations – what seems like laziness, an indifference toward work, an antipathy toward education – are really the results of economic and political circumstances that have been foisted upon Indians. If you live in a place where there are no jobs and no access to capital, not working becomes the norm. Any entrepreneurial impulse you have is quickly squelched. If you live in a place where the only jobs to be had are publicly funded and given out as rewards by political leaders, then nepotism (and the resulting corruption) becomes the norm. If you live in a place where the people who become schoolteachers are there because they're related to someone in tribal government, you start to lose respect for educational enterprises. If students who fail classes end up graduating anyway because of their family connections, school starts to seem pointless. And if you do work hard in school but find that it gets you nowhere afterward, you and the people around you start to wonder what the point of education is at all. In other words, Indians, just like all people, respond to the economic incentives and political conditions around them.

The effects of the current system, though, aren't only political and economic – why bother trying to extract natural resources from the ground or start your own business when you know it'll be decades before you see the fruits of your labor? – but also deeply emotional. People are tired, and they're bitter. They've tried to find a way out of their circumstances. But they're thwarted at every turn. Whether it's because they can't buy or sell their land outright, whether it's because they must ask the federal government's permission for things that other Americans take for granted, or whether it's because they've been relegated to the worst public schools, Indians can't seem to catch a break. And every time it seems as if they've found a way out – casinos, tax-free cigarettes – the federal government steps in and takes it away. Who can live like this?

The solutions offered by politicians, both tribal and federal, seem obvious – what Indians need is more money. But the trend of downward mobility seen on some of these reservations suggests that throwing more money at this problem isn't the answer. The sentiment that things used to be better in Indian country is more than simple nostalgia. In the case of the Lumbee community, the older generation really did receive a better education. These older men and women are now raising children whose parents have dropped out of school and dropped out of any kind of productive life. On the Crow and Northern Cheyenne reservations, there are fewer businesses than in decades past. And crime has become more frequent.

If there is a cultural problem, it's the culture of dependency that the federal government and the tribal governments have created. Whether it's money from Washington to pay for housing or food or fuel costs, or whether it's annuities coming from gaming endeavors, it has caused more problems than it has solved. And these funds haven't done much to alleviate the suffering of individual Indians. Except for the wealthiest of the casino owners, most Indians still live in poverty, with little access to good education, health care, or jobs. The lock-in weekend at the elementary school on Pine Ridge, prompted by the abuse that arises when government checks are spent on alcohol, suggests that people on reservations know exactly where the problems lie and how to stop them.

It's true that even though individuals have suffered, tribes have become more powerful as a result of the money flowing to them. As David Kimelberg, the Seneca Holdings CEO, points out, no one in Washington would be able to flood Seneca lands now as they did 50 years ago. The legal defense that Senecas would be able to mount would be much too powerful, thanks to the casino revenue filling their coffers.

But amassing political clout isn't enough. It's not enough for the individual Indians who live in difficult – sometimes destitute – conditions. The leaders of Indian nations often mean well. They believe that more revenue will fix their schools, their homes, and even their families. But it hasn't. When the federal government allocates money for reservations, that money becomes mired in the Bureau of Indian Affairs. Even now that it's run almost entirely by Indians, the BIA still doesn't behave responsibly. And even when the money gets to the tribes, so much of it seems to fall through the cracks. Meanwhile the involvement of the federal government has meant that individual initiative seems to be quashed completely. As one Crow legislator said, Indians are the most overregulated race on the planet.

But those Indians who do favor more individual responsibility and less dependency, who want Washington out of their lives but also want to create a private economy and alternatives to the tribal school systems, frequently face opposition from tribal leaders. For posing a threat to the status quo, people like Ben Chavis are often tarred as traitors to their race. Schools like Saint Labre and Red Cloud are dismissed as "too white," despite the fact that they do a better job of educating Indian kids. And representatives of Teach for America are branded as having "a savior mentality," even when they go out of their way to recruit Indian teachers.

For some Indian leaders, the status quo is simply not acceptable. People like Manny Jules have made it their mission to change the way Indians are treated by the Canadian government, but he too has been criticized as being too quick to assimilate. And his plan for the First Nations Property Ownership legislation has made other tribal leaders question his intentions.

All of this has the effect of ensuring that ordinary Indians don't rock the boat. From an economic standpoint as well as a political one, there's nothing to be gained from speaking up. The only Indian voices that most Americans hear are the ones of the political leadership. And that too is a problem.

American Indians make up the largest ethnic minority group in four states – Montana, North Dakota, Oklahoma, and South Dakota. These are the places where Indians represent a large enough population that politicians have to be truly responsive to the demands of the leadership. But the leadership isn't demanding reform. It's demanding more money.

The politicians representing those states – like those in other states – have a clear directive: bring home the bacon. Their goals in Washington are mostly to figure out how to get funding for programs that help people from their state. They're not being sent to Washington to reform the Bureau of Indian Affairs or introduce legislation that would clarify property rights on the reservation. They're not in Congress to try to get the courts to fix the jurisdictional ambiguities that make law enforcement on reservations a nightmare.

As mentioned in chapter 1, American Indians make up 1.7 percent of the U.S. population, according to the 2010 census. Their median age is under 30 and about seven years below the median for the population as a whole. And their numbers are projected to grow significantly, to 8.6 million by July 2050, when they might compose as much as 2 percent of the population.[20]

From a political perspective, this means that the problems of American Indians are growing as well. We can't assume there'll be some mass exodus from reservations. And we can't assume that politicians are going to work to solve these problems.

So what *can* we do? At one end of the spectrum, solutions to the problems of Indian reservations might require rethinking reservations altogether. As William Allen, former member of the U.S. Civil Rights Commission, suggests, the only way to give Indians the sovereignty to take control of their economic and political destinies, while ensuring that Indians enjoy all the protections of American citizens, is to make reservations into states. This would never be feasible for smaller tribes and smaller reservations, but Allen is right that under current law these semi-autonomous entities and the people who live within their borders are prevented from succeeding.

It would be hard to overstate the political obstacles to creating new states – are Montana and South Dakota going to voluntarily give up their land? – but there are solutions short of statehood that might help. The question of whether the First Nations Property Ownership Act being seriously considered in Canada can work in the United States is a useful one. Manny Jules and his colleagues aren't asking for the creation of new provinces to accommodate them. They see reserve land, for these purposes, as becoming more like cities. The underlying title would be turned over to a separate governing entity, and even when the land was sold, it'd remain part of the city, just as no one can sell a part of New York City to Newark. But individuals would be able to buy and sell it among themselves, without the permission or oversight of tribal or federal officials. Whether property reform can work in Canada remains to be seen and is a complicated question because of the treaties and agreements that most tribes have with the Canadian

government, not to mention the centuries of legal precedent governing these matters.

The reforms that are possible – given the political will to change
things – are at the bureaucratic level. Despite numerous attempts, no
one has yet been able to change the Bureau of Indian Affairs. If Terry
Anderson is right and the BIA has succeeded in creating more and
more regulations in order to perpetuate the need for its existence,
reforms will be very hard to institute. To change things will require
real oversight from Congress and the secretary of the interior. But it
will also require transparency. It's hard to shock the American people
with reports of wasteful spending in Washington. They've come to
expect it. But in this case, the spending is actually helping create economic problems for many Indians.

Perhaps one of the easiest problems for the public to understand is
the problem of law enforcement. The competing claims of jurisdiction when it comes to investigating and prosecuting criminals on
Indian lands have contributed to lawlessness on many reservations
and the suffering of their most vulnerable citizens. In principle, this is
a problem that law enforcement agencies deal with all the time – off
reservations, too. The question of whether the FBI, the state police, or
local authorities should be asked to handle a particular crime isn't
unique. What is unique, though, are the political and cultural sensi-
tivities on reservations. Federal and state authorities don't want to suggest that tribal authorities aren't doing a good job of policing their
own communities. And they're certainly reluctant to report or publi-
cize the more heinous crimes occurring on some reservations. But the
time has come for some honesty. Firing or threatening federal employees for reporting on child abuse or rape is unacceptable. And covering
up these problems will only make them worse.

Whether the cause of these crimes is the boarding-school experience of Indian parents or grandparents or some other factor not being
considered, the cycle has to stop somewhere. Attempts to deflect the
blame – by suggesting, for instance, that non-Indians are responsible
for the bulk of these misdeeds, coming onto Indian land to assault and

rape – are dishonest and do a great disservice to the victims. Federal agencies should be reporting on these matters correctly, and the media has a duty to uncover the worst abuses, even if that means there may be politically incorrect conclusions to their articles.

Laws and lawmakers who continue to protect the tribe even over the interests of individual Indians must be reconsidered. The Indian Child Welfare Act, which was conceived as a way of protecting Indian children, has become a way of increasing the rolls of tribal membership even at the expense of finding a decent home for a child. Unlike for some of the other reforms discussed in this book, there's a coalition of people who could potentially lobby Congress for changes to ICWA, including adoption agencies and civil rights organizations. In the summer of 2015, the Arizona-based Goldwater Institute filed a class-action lawsuit to challenge the constitutionality of ICWA.

The final area of reform – education – holds the most potential for improving the lives of American Indians. With few exceptions, the schools that Indian children attend look no different from the schools in our worst inner cities. They're plagued by a lack of discipline, under-qualified teachers, crumbling facilities, and a lack of parental involvement. Despite spending more per pupil than schools nearby, they produce graduates who are unprepared for college or a career. Again, there's nothing surprising about this. The school administrations and teachers serve the whims of tribal leadership. The education system has been politicized. Not only do parents typically have no choice about where to send their kids, but because many Indian communities are so isolated, parents may not even be aware that a better option exists.

Because education reform is currently happening all over the country, it's possible to find different models for success. Just as teachers' unions and the politicians they support don't want to see fundamental changes in failing public school systems, so the tribal powers that be may not want to see these kind of reforms.

But there's tremendous potential here. A few Catholic schools have long been an alternative to the public-school models on these reservations. But they depend on outside donations. And it's hard to imagine that they'll be able to replicate themselves any time soon. Still, their stories need to be told, so that more parents on reservations can begin to understand there are alternatives.

Young men and women who come to reservations through Teach for America have clearly been a boon to reservation schools. Parents, more often than not, are thrilled to see these teachers at the front of their children's classrooms. But tribal leaders view outsiders such as TFA corps members with suspicion, and principals will fire them at the drop of a hat. It's hard to imagine that TFA is anything but a temporary fix for a crippling problem.

Still, when parents do see how much a qualified teacher can really offer their kids, it may whet the community's appetite for reform. The most promising alternatives for education reform in Indian communities are probably charter schools. Only by witnessing high-performing charter schools educating impoverished kids hundreds of miles away can parents on reservations even begin to understand what they're missing. If states like South Dakota had the support of Indians in passing a charter law, the results would be obvious immediately. The increase in competition would have an immediate impact even on children who didn't attend the new schools. What these communities need are schools that are truly disconnected from the political process, where jobs and grades are awarded not on the basis of family connections but on the basis of merit. Creating a generation of well-educated adults might go a long way toward fixing problems that seem intractable now.

While touring America in the 1830s, French statesman Alexis de Tocqueville spent time observing the state of American Indians, particularly their moves to reservations and the resulting deprivations:

> *It is impossible to conceive the frightful sufferings that attend these forced migrations. They are undertaken by a people already exhausted and reduced; and the countries to which the new-comers betake*

themselves are inhabited by other tribes, which receive them with jealous hostility. Hunger is in the rear, war awaits them, and misery besets them on all sides. To escape from so many enemies, they separate, and each individual endeavors to procure secretly the means of supporting his existence by isolating himself, living in the immensity of the desert like an outcast in civilized society. The social tie, which distress had long since weakened, is then dissolved; they have no longer a country, and soon they will not be a people; their very families are obliterated; their common name is forgotten; their language perishes; and all traces of their origin disappear.[21]

Tocqueville warns his 19th-century readers that he's not overstating the case: "I should be sorry to have my reader suppose that I am coloring the picture too highly; I saw with my own eyes many of the miseries that I have just described, and was the witness of sufferings that I have not the power to portray."

Despite his obvious sympathy for their plight, or perhaps because of it, he went on to predict a dire fate: "I believe that the Indian nations of North America are doomed to perish, and that whenever the Europeans shall be established on the shores of the Pacific Ocean, that race of men will have ceased to exist. The Indians had only the alternative of war or civilization; in other words, they must either destroy the Europeans or become their equals."

This seems to be one of the few cases in which the great French traveler was proved wrong. Indians have not perished. Nor, obviously, did they destroy the Europeans. But they've been left in a kind of limbo, their communities existing in a kind of suspended animation. The reservation system didn't destroy them, but it did render them powerless over their own economic and political destiny. Non-Indian Americans like to think of themselves as much more enlightened than their predecessors when it comes to Indians, but our current policies aren't much better than those of almost 200 years ago. Indians, as any visitor to a reservation can see, have chosen civilization; now it's time for America to make them equal Americans.

ACKNOWLEDGMENTS

When people ask me how I came to write a book about American Indians, I can only say anger. For years, I had read about the poverty, suicide, abuse, and alcohol and drug problems on reservations with a deep sense of sadness. I had assumed, as many readers had, that little could be done about these problems. But when I attended a conference at the Property and Environment Research Center in 2013, it became clear that things were both more and less hopeless than I had imagined.

The people I met there – a group of incredibly smart, tenacious professors, leaders, and reformers – had spent their lives fighting for their people to fix a broken system in the face of long odds. I am indebted to Terry Anderson for allowing me to be a part of that group.

Meeting and getting to know Ivan Small, Ben Chavis, Manny Jules, and André Le Dressay has been a rare privilege, and I cannot thank them enough for the time they spent with me and the efforts they expended to show me their hardest problems and their best solutions. I can only hope I have told their stories with the care they deserve.

This project would not have been possible without the support of the Searle Trust and the Randolph Foundation. I am deeply grateful to Kim Dennis and Heather Higgins, who trusted me with this sensitive and vexing topic.

And I am deeply grateful to my family. This book has been informed by a deep love and respect for American history, politics, and culture that my parents instilled in me from a young age. I hope that I can pass on some of that to my children. In the meantime, I thank Emily, Simon, and Leah for their patience and love. And thanks above all to my husband Jason, my best critic and my best friend.

NOTES

INTRODUCTION

1   Suzanne Macartney, Alemayehu Bishaw, and Kayla Fontenot, *Poverty Rates for Selected Detailed Race and Hispanic Groups by State and Place:* 2007–2011 (Washington, D.C.: U.S. Census Bureau, 2013), http://www.census.gov/prod/2013pubs/acsbr11-17.pdf.

2   Center for Native American Youth, *Native American Youth* 101: *Information on the Historical Context and Current Status of Indian Country and Native American Youth* (Washington, D.C.: The Aspen Institute, n.d.), http://www.aspeninstitute.org/sites/default/files/content/upload/Native%20American%20Youth%20101_higres.pdf.

3   Karen Chartier and Raul Caetano, "Ethnicity and Health Disparities in Alcohol Research," http://pubs.niaaa.nih.gov/publications/arh40/152-160.htm.

4   Center for Native American Youth, *Native American Youth* 101.

5   Patricia Tjaden and Nancy Thoennes, *Extent, Nature, and Consequences of Rape Victimization: Findings from the National Violence against Women Survey* (Washington, D.C.: National Institute of Justice, 2006), https://www.ncjrs.gov/pdffiles1/nij/210346.pdf.

6   Lawrence A. Greenfield and Steven K. Smith, *American Indians and Crime* (Washington, D.C.: Bureau of Justice Statistics, 1999), http://bjs.gov/content/pub/pdf/aic.pdf.

7   Jane Palmer, "Native Americans," in *Sexual Violence and Abuse: An Encyclopedia of Prevention, Impacts, and Recovery*, ed. Judy Postmus (Santa Barbara: ABC-CLIO, 2012).

8   Chris Edwards, "Indian Lands, Indian Subsidies, and the Bureau of Indian Affairs," http://www.downsizinggovernment.org/interior/indian-lands-indian-subsidies.

9   National Center for Education Statistics, "How Much Money Does the United States Spend on Public Elementary and Secondary Schools?" https://nces.ed.gov/fastfacts/display.asp?id=66.

10 Edwards, "Indian Lands."

NOTES

11 Emma Brown, "Washington Is Taking Notice of Crumbling Native American Schools," *Washington Post*, May 19, 2015, http://www.washingtonpost.com/local/education/native-american-schools-long-have-been-crumbling-but-now-washington-is-paying-attention/2015/05/19/717560fe-fd6c-11e4-805c-c3f407e5a9e9_story.html.

12 Alysa Landry, "'All Indians Are Dead?' At Least That's What Most Schools Teach Children," Indian Country Today Media Network, November 17, 2014, http://indiancountrytodaymedianetwork.com/2014/11/17/all-indians-are-dead-least-thats-what-most-schools-teach-children-157822.

13 "The Navajos: The Long Walk and the Escape to Utah," http://www.utahindians.org/Curriculum/pdf/HSnavajo.pdf.

14 Fergus M. Bordewich, *Killing the White Man's Indian: Reinventing Native Americans at the End of the Twentieth Century* (New York: Doubleday, 1996), p. 132.

CHAPTER ONE

1 United States Senate Committee on Indian Affairs Field Oversight Hearing, Crow Agency, MT, Empowering Indian Country: Coal, Jobs, and Self-Determination, April 8, 2015, http://www.indian.senate.gov/sites/default/files/upload/files/4.6.2015%20SCIA%20Witness%20Testimony%20-%20Eric%20Henson.pdf.

2 Timothy Williams, "Higher Crime, Fewer Charges on Indian Land," *New York Times*, February 20, 2012, http://www.nytimes.com/2012/02/21/us/on-indian-reservations-higher-crime-and-fewer-prosecutions.html.

3 Edwards, "Indian Lands."

4 Terry L. Anderson, *Sovereign Nations or Reservations? An Economic History of American Indians* (San Francisco: Pacific Research Institute for Public Policy, 1995), p. 14.

5 Francis Paul Prucha, *The Great Father: The United States Government and the American Indians*, abridged ed. (Lincoln: University of Nebraska Press, 1986), p. 243.

6 David H. Thomas, *Skull Wars: Kennewick Man, Archaeology, and the Battle for Native American Identity* (New York: Basic Books, 2001), p. 42.

7 Ibid.

8 Charles Glenn, *American Indian/First Nations Schooling: From the Colonial Period to the Present* (New York: Palgrave Macmillan, 2011), p. 26.

9 Bordewich, *Killing the White Man's Indian*, p. 280.

10 Ibid., p. 117.

11 Ibid., p. 120.

12 Ibid., p. 121.

13 *An Act to Provide for the Allotment of Lands in Severalty to Indians on the Various Reservations (General Allotment Act or Dawes Act), Statutes at Large* 24, 388-91, NADP Document A1887, http://public.csusm.edu/nadp/a1887.htm.

14 "Dawes Act (1887)," http://www.ourdocuments.gov/doc.php?doc=50.

15   Indian Land Tenure Foundation, "History of Allotment," https://www.iltf.org/resources/land-tenure-history/allotment.

16   Anderson, *Sovereign Nations or Reservations?* p. 97.

17   John Koppisch, "Why Are Indian Reservations So Poor? A Look at the Bottom 1%," *Forbes*, December 13, 2011, http://www.forbes.com/sites/johnkoppisch/2011/12/13/why-are-indian-reservations-so-poor-a-look-at-the-bottom-1.

18   Ibid.

19   Terry Anderson, "Self-Determination – The Other Path for Native Americans," *PERC Report* 4, no. 22 (2006), http://www.perc.org/articles/self-determination.

20   Ibid.

21   Charles Mann, 1491: *New Revelations of the Americas before Columbus* (New York: Knopf, 2005), pp. 308–9.

22   *United States v. Washington*, 384 F. Supp. 312 (W.D. Wash. 1974), http://dspace.library.colostate.edu/webclient/DeliveryManager/digitool_items/cub01_storage/2012/10/22/file_1/172443.

23   Bordewich, *Killing the White Man's Indian*, p. 118.

24   Leonard A. Carlson, *Indians, Bureaucrats, and Land: The Dawes Act and the Decline of Indian Farming* (Westport, CT: Greenwood Press, 1981), p. 174.

25   Anderson, *Sovereign Nations or Reservations?* p. 108.

26   Ibid., p. 97.

27   Ibid., p. 106.

28   Bordewich, *Killing the White Man's Indian*, p. 124.

29   PLACE Advocacy, *Guide to Homesite Leases* (Bozeman, MT: Author, n.d.), http://placeadvocacy.org/lease.pdf.

30   Shawn E. Regan and Terry L. Anderson, "The Energy Wealth of Indian Nations," *LSU Journal of Energy Law and Resources* 3, no. 1 (2014), p. 2. http://digitalcommons.law.lsu.edu/jelr/vol3/iss1/9.

31   George W. Bush Institute, Executive Summary of "The Energy Wealth of Indian Nations" by Shawn E. Regan and Terry L. Anderson, http://www.bushcenter.org/sites/default/files/GWBI-EnergyWealthIndianNations.pdf3 LSU J. of Energy L. & Resources (2014), http://digitalcommons.law.lsu.edu/jelr/vol3/iss1/9.

32   Edwards, "Indian Lands" (see introduction, n. 8).

33   Dan Frosch, "Pulling Aid Away, Shutdown Deepens Indians' Distress," *New York Times*, October 13, 2013, http://www.nytimes.com/2013/10/14/us/pulling-aid-away-shutdown-deepens-indians-distress.html.

34   Ibid.

35   First Nations Tax Commission, "Research: Expanding Commercial Activity on First Nation Lands," http://www.fiscalrealities.com/uploads/1/0/7/1/10716604/expanding_commercial_activity.pdf.

36   "Remarks by the First Lady at White House Tribal Youth Gathering," The White House, Office of the First Lady, July 9, 2015, https://www.whitehouse.gov/the-press-office/2015/07/09/remarks-first-lady-white-house-tribal-youth-gathering.

37 Larry Schweikart, "Buffaloed: The Myth and Reality of Bison in America," *Free-man*, December 1, 2002, http://fee.org/freeman/buffaloed-the-myth-and-reality-of-bison-in-america.

38 Ibid.

39 Jen St. Denis, "Manny Jules: Taxing Times," *Business in Vancouver*, April 29, 2013, https://www.biv.com/article/2013/4/manny-jules-taxing-times.

40 Kathy Brock, "One Source, Two Tributaries of Aboriginal-State Relations," in *Canada and the United States: Differences That Count*, 4th ed., ed. David M. Thomas and David N. Biette (North York, ON: University of Toronto Press, 2014), p. 364.

41 Ibid., p. 365.

42 *"Calder v. Attorney General of British Columbia* (1970)." *American Indian History Online*. Facts on File, Inc. http://www.fofweb.com/History/MainPrintPage.asp?iPin=ind6552&DataType=Indian&WinType=Free.

43 Thalassa Research Associates, "The Douglas Reserve Policy," http://gsdl.ubcic.bc.ca/collect/specific/index/assoc/HASH9161.dir/doc.doc.

44 Mark Milke, *Incomplete, Illiberal, and Expensive: A Review of 15 Years of Treaty Negotiations in British Columbia and Proposals for Reform* (Vancouver, BC: Fraser Institute, 2008), http://www.fraserinstitute.org/sites/default/files/15_Years_BC_Treaty_NegotiationsRev2.pdf.

45 Fraser Institute, "Flawed Process for BC Treaty Negotiations Costing Billions of Dollars with No End in Sight," (press release), July 28, 2008, http://www.marketwired.com/press-release/fraser-institute-flawed-process-bc-treaty-negotiations-costing-billions-dollars-with-883131.htm.

46 Ibid.

47 Tsilhqot'in Nation *v.* British Columbia, 2014 SCC 44, [2014] 2 S.C.R. 256, https://scc-csc.lexum.com/scc-csc/scc-csc/en/item/14246/index.do.

48 Tom Flanagan, Christopher Alcantara, and André Le Dressay, *Beyond the Indian Act: Restoring Aboriginal Property Rights* (Montreal: McGill-Queen's University Press, 2010), p. 3.

49 U.S. Census Bureau, "American Indian and Alaska Native Heritage Month: November 2011," https://www.census.gov/newsroom/releases/archives/facts_for_features_special_editions/cb11-ff22.html.

50 Aboriginal Affairs and Northern Development Canada, *Aboriginal Demographics from the 2011 National Household Survey* (N.p.: Author, 2013), https://www.aadnc-aandc.gc.ca/eng/1370438978311/1370439050610#chp2.

51 Mark Kennedy, "First Nations: 'Time Bomb' Is Ticking, New Book Argues," *Ottawa Citizen*, December 6, 2014, http://ottawacitizen.com/news/politics/first-nations-time-bomb-is-ticking-new-book-argues.

52 "To Sir Wilfrid Laurier, Premier of the Dominion of Canada, From the Chiefs of the Shuswap, Okanagan and Couteau Tribes of British Columbia. Presented at Kamloops, B.C. August 25, 1910" (letter), http://shuswapnation.org/wordpress/wp-content/uploads/2012/09/1910-SIR-WILFRID-LAURIER-MEMORIAL.pdf.

53 Flanagan, Alcantara, and Le Dressay, *Beyond the Indian Act*, p. 41.

54 S.C. Gwynne, *Empire of the Summer Moon: Quanah Parker and the Rise and Fall of the Comanches, the Most Powerful Indian Tribe in American History* (New York: Simon and Schuster, 2010), p. 319.

55 Ibid.

CHAPTER TWO

1   Michael Sokolove, "Foxwoods Is Fighting for Its Life," *New York Times Magazine*, March 14, 2012, http://www.nytimes.com/2012/03/18/magazine/mike-sokolove-foxwood-casinos.html.

2   Ronald Johnson, "Indian Casinos: Another Tragedy of the Commons," in *Self-Determination: The Other Path for Native Americans*, ed. Terry L. Anderson, Bruce L. Benson, and Thomas E. Flanagan (Stanford, CA: Stanford University Press, 2006), p. 238.

3   Glenn Blain, "Gov. Cuomo Says Casinos Will Bring Jobs to Upstate Communities," *New York Daily News*, December 18, 2014, http://www.nydailynews.com/blogs/dailypolitics/gov-cuomo-casinos-bring-jobs-upstate-blog-entry-1.2050110.

4   Niels Lesniewski, "Begich Slams McCaskill in Feud over Alaska Native Corporations," *#WGDB* (blog), *Roll Call*, July 2, 2014, http://blogs.rollcall.com/wgdb/begich-mccaskill-spar-over-alaska-native-corporations-again.

5   Paul C. Rosier, "Dam Building and Treaty Breaking: The Kinzua Dam Controversy, 1936–1958," *Pennsylvania Magazine of History and Biography* 119, no. 4 (1995): pp. 345–68, https://journals.psu.edu/pmhb/article/view/45031/44752.

6   Michael L. Ross, "Does Oil Hinder Democracy?" (abstract), *World Politics* 53, no. 3 (2001): pp. 325–61, http://journals.cambridge.org/action/displayAbstract?from Page=online&aid=7678284&fileId=S0043887100020153.

7   Robert D. McFadden, "Seneca Feud Boils Over; 3 Are Slain," *New York Times*, March 26, 1995, http://www.nytimes.com/1995/03/26/nyregion/seneca-feud-boils-over-3-are-slain.html.

8   John Kifner, "Tribal Shootout: Rival Factions behind Conflict," *New York Times*, April 3, 1995, http://www.nytimes.com/1995/04/03/nyregion/tribal-shootout-rival-factions-behind-conflict.html.

9   Stephanie Woodard, "Oglala Sioux Tribal Council Takes Aim at Newspaper, Attorney," *Indian Country Today Media Network*, March 31, 2015, http://indiancountry todaymedianetwork.com/2015/03/31/oglala-sioux-tribal-council-takes-aim-news paper-attorney-159837.

10 Tom Dennis, "Our Opinion: Real Reform on Reservations Starts with a Free Press," *Grand Forks Herald*, June 17, 2014, http://www.grandforksherald.com/content/our-opinion-real-reform-reservations-starts-free-press.

11 Cynthia Hess and Claudia Williams, *The Status of Women in Robeson County, North Carolina* (Washington, D.C.: Institute for Women's Policy Research, 2013), available

at http://www.iwpr.org/publications/pubs/the-status-of-women-in-robeson-county-north-carolina.

12   "3-Year-Old Drowns in Robeson County Drainage Ditch," February 16, 2010, http://www.wral.com/news/local/story/7053287.

13   Dr. Jack Campisi's testimony before the Committee on Indian Affairs, legislative hearing on S. 660, July 12, 2006, http://www.indian.senate.gov/sites/default/files/upload/files/Campisi071206.pdf.

14   Bordewich, *Killing the White Man's Indian*, p. 75.

15   Ibid., p. 63.

16   Ben Chavis, *Crazy Like a Fox: One Principal's Triumph in the Inner City* (New York: Penguin, 2010), p. 138.

17   H.R. 184, 114th Cong. (2015), https://www.congress.gov/114/bills/hr184/BILLS-114hr184ih.xml.

18   "Hagan Makes Pitch for Lumbee," *Robesonian*, July 20, 2015, https://robesonian.com/archive/11789/news-home_top-news-2770407-hagan-makes-pitch-for-lumbee.

19   Ibid.

CHAPTER THREE

1   Erik Eckholm, "Gang Violence Grows on an Indian Reservation," *New York Times*, December 13, 2009, http://www.nytimes.com/2009/12/14/us/14gangs.html.

2   Trymaine Lee and Peter van Agtmael, "Law and Disorder on the Pine Ridge Indian Reservation," MSNBC.com, May 29, 2014, http://www.msnbc.com/msnbc/law-disorder-pine-ridge-indian-reservation.

3   Lesli A. Maxwell, "Education in Indian Country: Running in Place," *Education Week*, December 4, 2013, http://www.edweek.org/ew/projects/2013/native-american-education/running-in-place.html.

4   Joyce Riha Linik, "Working Together to Help Indian Youth Succeed: Big Sky Hope," *Education Northwest Magazine*, Spring–Summer 2011, pp. 24–29, http://opi.mt.gov/PDF/Promise/ednwmag_sp-su11_big-sky-hope.pdf.

5   U.S. Census Bureau, Educational Finance Branch, *Public Education Finances: 2013* (2015), https://www.census.gov/content/dam/Census/library/publications/2015/econ/g13-aspef.pdf.

6   Sarah Butrymowicz, "The Failure of Tribal Schools," *Atlantic*, November 26, 2014, http://www.theatlantic.com/education/archive/2014/11/the-failure-of-tribal-schools/383211.

7   Sarah Butrymowicz, "Tribal Colleges Give Poor Return on More Than $100 Million a Year in Federal Money," *Hechinger Report*, http://hechingerreport.org/tribal-colleges-give-poor-return-100-million-year-federal-money.

8   "Seneca Allegany Charter School Letter of Intent," http://www.p12.nysed.gov/psc/documents/SenecaAlleganyLoIRedacted.pdf.

9   http://www.p12.nysed.gov/psc/documents/SenecaAlleganyRedacted.pdf.

10   Stuart Buck, *Acting White: The Ironic Legacy of Desegregation* (New Haven, CT: Yale University Press, 2010).

11   http://www.ncreportcards.org/src/servlet/srcICreatePDF?pSchCode=420&pLEAC ode=780&pYear=2012-2013.

12   Emma Brown, "Obama Budget Includes $1 Billion for Native American Education," *Washington Post*, January 30, 2015, http://www.washingtonpost.com/local/ education/obama-budget-includes-1-billion-for-native-american-education/2015/ 01/30/10785b08-a8a8-11e4-a2b2-776095f393b2_story.html.

13   Rishawn Biddle, "BIE's Fiscal Failure of Native Kids," *Dropout Nation*, November 18, 2014, http://dropoutnation.net/2014/11/18/bies-fiscal-failure-of-native-kids.

CHAPTER FOUR

1   "Public Schools of Robeson County, North Carolina," Ballotpedia: The Encyclopedia of American Politics, http://ballotpedia.org/Public_Schools_of_Robeson_ County,_North_Carolina.

2   *Washington Post*, "America's Most Challenging High Schools: Top 100," April 7, 2014, https://www.washingtonpost.com/apps/g/page/local/americas-most-challeng ing-high-schools-top-100/915.

3   Andrew J. Coulson, "OUSD Made Wrong Decision to Close American Indian Charter Schools," Cato Institute, http://www.cato.org/publications/commentary/ ousd-made-wrong-decision-close-american-indian-charter-schools.

4   National Alliance for Public Charter Schools, *Measuring Up to the Model: A Ranking of State Charter School Laws*, 3rd ed. (Washington, D.C.: Author, 2012), http:// www.publiccharters.org/wp-content/uploads/2014/01/NAPCS_2012_StateLawRank ings_Final_20120117T162953.pdf.

5   "St. Labre Indian School: Culture," Saint Labre Indian School, http://www.stlabre. org/discover/culture/culture.html.

6   St. Labre Indian School, "About Us," http://www.stlabre.org/about-us.

7   William Marino, "St. Labre Indian School Continues 127-Year Heritage of Service to Native American People of SE Montana" (press release), March 24, 2011, http:// www.prweb.com/releases/2011/03/prweb5193204.htm.

8   Jan Falstad, "Church, School Sued by Tribe," *Billings Gazette*, March 11, 2005, http://billingsgazette.com/news/local/church-school-sued-by-tribe/article_58c3cc40-22fe-5480-a5ba-acdb7ac87b76.html.

9   Mark Yapching, "Crow Nation Native American Reservation Declares 'Jesus Christ Is Lord,'" *Christian Today*, January 23, 2015, http://www.christiantoday.com/ article/crow.nation.native.american.reservation.declares.jesus.christ.is.lord/466 23.htm.

10   *Official Report of the Nineteenth Annual Conference of Charities and Correction* (1892), 46–59, reprinted in Richard H. Pratt, "The Advantages of Mingling Indians with Whites," *Americanizing the American Indians: Writings by the "Friends of the Indian"*

1880–1900 (Cambridge, MA: Harvard University Press, 1973), pp. 260–271, retrieved from http://historymatters.gmu.edu/d/4929.

11 "A History of Residential Schools in Canada," CBC News, May 16, 2008, http://www.cbc.ca/news/canada/a-history-of-residential-schools-in-canada-1.702280.

12 Ibid.

13 Ibid.

14 Teach for America press kit, https://www.teachforamerica.org/sites/default/files/2014-15teach-for-america-press-kit.pdf.

15 Valerie Strauss, "Why Teach for America Can't Recruit in My Classroom," *Answer Sheet* (blog), *Washington Post*, February 18, 2013, http://www.washingtonpost.com/blogs/answer-sheet/wp/2013/02/18/professor-why-teach-for-america-cant-recruit-in-my-classroom.

16 "Teach for America Welcomes Most Diverse Talent in 25-Year History" (press release), August 11, 2014, https://www.teachforamerica.org/about-us/media-resources/news-releases/teach-america-welcomes-most-diverse-talent-25-year-history.

17 "The Ruth Danley & William Enoch Moore Fund," Foundation Directory Online, last updated December 29, 2014, https://fdo.foundationcenter.org/grantmaker-profile?collection=grantmakers&key=DANL003&page=7&from_search=1.

18 *Native News Online* Staff, "Unprecedented Accomplishments on the Pine Ridge Reservation," *Native News Online*, January 31, 2014, http://nativenewsonline.net/education/unprecedented-accomplishments-pine-ridge-reservation.

19 "Ways to Give," Red Cloud Indian School, https://www.redcloudschool.org/waystogive.

CHAPTER FIVE

1 Adoptive Couple v. Baby Girl, 133 S. Ct. 2552 (2013), https://scholar.google.com/scholar_case?case=4067130190123998757&hl=en&as_sdt=6&as_vis=1&oi=scholar.

2 Ibid.

3 Joe Flood, "What's Lurking behind the Suicides?" *New York Times Sunday Review*, May 16, 2015, http://www.nytimes.com/2015/05/17/opinion/sunday/whats-lurking-behind-the-suicides.html.

4 Laurel Morales, "Many Native American Communities Struggle with Effects of Heroin Use," *Morning Edition*, NPR, May 20, 2015, http://www.npr.org/2015/05/20/405936140/many-native-american-communities-struggle-with-effects-of-heroin-use.

5 Timothy Williams, "A Tribe's Epidemic of Child Sex Abuse, Minimized for Years," *New York Times*, September 19, 2012, http://www.nytimes.com/2012/09/20/us/us-steps-in-as-child-sex-abuse-pervades-sioux-tribe.html.

6 Timothy Williams, "Psychologist Who Wrote of Abuse Is Punished," *New York Times*, July 30, 2012, http://www.nytimes.com/2012/07/31/us/doctor-who-warned-of-spirit-lake-abuse-is-reprimanded.html.

7   Ibid.

8   Timothy Williams, "Official Rescinds Punishment of Psychologist on Reservation," *New York Times*, August 2, 2012, http://www.nytimes.com/2012/08/03/us/spirit-lake-psychologists-punishment-rescinded.html.

9   Sarah Childress, "Man Convicted of Child Abuse at Spirit Lake Reservation," PBS. org, March 29, 2013, http://www.pbs.org/wgbh/pages/frontline/biographies/kind-hearted-woman/man-convicted-of-child-abuse-at-spirit-lake-reservation.

10   "13th Mandated Report re: Spirit Lake Child Abuse" (blog entry), Christian Alliance for Indian Child Welfare, April 5, 2013, http://caicw.org/tag/senator-hoeven.

11   "Rotherham Child Abuse Scandal: 1,400 Children Exploited, Report Finds," BBC News, August 26, 2014, http://www.bbc.com/news/uk-england-south-yorkshire-28939089.

12   Roger Scruton, "Why Did British Police Ignore Pakistani Gangs Abusing 1,400 Rotherham Children? Political Correctness," *Forbes*, August 30, 2014, http://www.forbes.com/sites/rogerscruton/2014/08/30/why-did-british-police-ignore-pakistani-gangs-raping-rotherham-children-political-correctness.

13   Gordon Rayner, "Denis MacShane: I Was Too Much of a 'Liberal Leftie' and Should Have Done More to Investigate Child Abuse," *Telegraph*, August 27, 2014, http://www.telegraph.co.uk/news/uknews/crime/11059643/Denis-MacShane-I-was-too-much-of-a-liberal-leftie-and-should-have-done-more-to-investigate-child-abuse.html.

14   Virginia L. Colin, *Infant Attachment: What We Know Now* (Washington, D.C.: U.S. Department of Health and Human Services, 1991), http://aspe.hhs.gov/basic-report/infant-attachment-what-we-know-now.

15   Jody Allen Crowe, *The Fatal Link: The Connection between School Shooters and the Brain Damage from Prenatal Exposure to Alcohol* (Denver: Outskirts Press, 2009), p. 8.

16   Ibid., p. 9.

17   U.S. Department of Health and Human Services, Substance Abuse and Mental Health Services Administration, Center for Substance Abuse Prevention, *Fetal Alcohol Spectrum Disorders among Native Americans* (Washington, D.C.: Author, 2007), http://fasdcenter.samhsa.gov/documents/NI_WYNTK_FASD_Among_AIAN.pdf.

18   U.S. Department of Justice, Office on Violence against Women, *FY 2016 Congressional Budget Submission*, http://www.justice.gov/sites/default/files/jmd/pages/attachments/2015/02/02/30._office_on_violence_against_women_ovw.pdf.

19   Sari Horwitz, "New Law Offers Protection to Abused Native American Women," *Washington Post*, February 8, 2014, https://www.washingtonpost.com/world/national-security/new-law-offers-a-sliver-of-protection-to-abused-native-american-women/2014/02/08/0466d1ae-8f73-11e3-84e1-27626c5ef5fb_story.html.

20   "Tribal Communities," U.S. Department of Justice, Office on Violence against Women, http://www.justice.gov/ovw/tribal-communities.

21   Laura Sullivan, "Rape Cases on Indian Lands Go Uninvestigated," *All Things Considered*, NPR, http://www.npr.org/templates/story/story.php?storyId=12203114.

22   Horwitz, "New Law."

23   U.S. Department of Justice, *Indian Country Investigations and Prosecutions:* 2013 (Washington, D.C.: Author, n.d.), http://www.justice.gov/sites/default/files/tribal/legacy/2014/08/26/icip-rpt-cy2013.pdf.

24   Larry Long, Rich Braunstein, Brenda Manning, and William Anderson, "Understanding Contextual Differences in American Indian Criminal Justice," *American Indian Culture and Research Journal* 32, no. 4 (2008), pp. 41–65, http://citation. allacademic.com/meta/p_mla_apa_research_citation/3/6/1/1/5/p361154_ index.html?phpsessid=0f7721197 10c5e0639550d0cfaf4a08e.

25   Ibid.

26   Horwitz, "New Law."

27   http://webcache.googleusercontent.com/search?q=cache:vuhCzQIbBhQJ:https:// www.nacdl.org/WorkArea/DownloadAsset.aspx%3Fid%3D24190%26libID%3D24 159+&cd=2&hl=en&ct=clnk&gl=us.

28   Santa Clara Pueblo v. Martinez, 436 US 49 - Supreme Court 1978, https://scholar. google.com/scholar_case?case=8956958372276107542&hl=en&as_sdt=6&as_ vis=1 &oi=scholar.

CONCLUSION

1   ICTMN Staff, "Quechan Skate Park Project Turns Down 'Bribe Money' From Redskins," *Indian Country Today Media Network,* July 17, 2014, http://indiancountrytodaymedianetwork.com/2014/07/17/quechan-skate-park-project-turns-down-bribe-money-redskins-155901.

2   Ibid.

3   Jeremy Stahl, "Native American Groups Ask Twitter, Facebook, and Google to Remove Washington NFL Accounts," *The Slatest* (blog), *Slate,* August 7, 2014, http://www.slate.com/blogs/the_slatest/2014/08/07/native_american_groups_ask_ twitter_facebook_and_google_to_remove_washington.html.

4   Ken Belson, "Obama Points to 'Legitimate Concerns' over Redskins' Name," *New York Times,* October 5, 2013, http://www.nytimes.com/2013/10/06/sports/football/ obama-enters-the-debate-on-the-redskins-name.html.

5   "Open Letter From Dan Snyder: The Washington Redskins Original Americans Foundation" (forum post), March 24, 2014, http://es.redskins.com/topic/377755-open-letter-from-dan-snyder-the-washington-redskins-original-americans-foundation.

6   Megan Finnerty, "Yuma Tribe Rejects Money from Redskins Owner's Foundation," *Republic,* azcentral.com, http://www.azcentral.com/story/news/arizona/2014/07/18/ yuma-tribe-rejects-money-redskins-owners-foundation/12823031.

7   National Congress of American Indians, *Ending the Legacy of Racism in Sports & the Era of Harmful "Indian" Sports Mascots* (Washington, D.C.: Author, 2013), http:// www.ncai.org/resources/ncai-publications/Ending_the_Legacy_of_Racism.pdf.

8   William Voegeli, "The Redskins and Their Offense," May 6, 2014, *Claremont Review of Books*, http://www.claremont.org/article/the-redskins-and-their-offense.

9   Victoria Cavaliere, "Seattle Lawmakers Vote to Change Name of Columbus Day Holiday," Reuters, October 6, 2014, http://www.reuters.com/article/2014/10/06/us-usa-washington-columbus-idUSKCN0HV27E20141006.

10 Drew DeSilver, "Working on Columbus Day? It Depends on Where You Live," Pew Research Center, October 8, 2015, http://www.pewresearch.org/fact-tank/2015/10/08/working-on-columbus-day-it-depends-on-where-you-live.

11 American Indian Movement Grand Governing Council, "Ward Churchill, Academic Fraud, Literary Fraud, and Indian Fraud" (press statement), July 26, 2007, http://www.aimovement.org/moipr/churchillpress.html.

12 Amy Goodman, "Challenging Columbus Day: Denver Organizers Discuss Why They Protest the Holiday," *Democracy Now!* October 6, 2006, http://www.democracynow.org/2006/10/6/challenging_columbus_day_denver_organizers_discuss.

13 Renee K. Gadoua, "Nuns to Pope: Revoke 15th-Century Doctrine That Allows Christians to Seize Native Land," Religion News Service, September 9, 2014, http://www.religionnews.com/2014/09/09/nuns-pope-revoke-15th-century-doctrine-allows-christians-seize-native-land.

14 Vimal Patel, "Why So Few American Indians Earn Ph.D.'s, and What Colleges Can Do about It," *Chronicle of Higher Education*, May 27, 2014, http://chronicle.com/article/Why-So-Few-American-Indians/146715.

15 Kelsey Sheehy, "Graduation Rates Dropping among Native American Students," *U.S. News and World Report*, June 6, 2013, http://www.usnews.com/education/high-schools/articles/2013/06/06/graduation-rates-dropping-among-native-american-students.

16 James Calvin Schaap, "The Dakota War of 1862: Part 2: The Use of Memory," Books & Culture: A Christian Review, http://www.booksandculture.com/articles/webexclusives/2012/august/dakota-war-of-1862.html.

17 Ibid.

18 Michelle Sarche and Paul Spicer, "Poverty and Health Disparities for American Indian and Alaska Native Children: Current Knowledge and Future Prospects," http://www.ncbi.nlm.nih.gov/pmc/articles/PMC2567901.

19 Kevin Gover (Pawnee), "American Indians Serve in the U.S. Military in Greater Numbers Than Any Ethnic Group and Have Since the Revolution," *National Museum of the American Indian* (blog), *Huffington Post*, May 22, 2015, http://www.huffingtonpost.com/national-museum-of-the-american-indian/american-indians-serve-in-the-us-military_b_7417854.html.

20 U.S. Census Bureau, "American Indian and Alaska Native Heritage Month: November 2011," https://www.census.gov/newsroom/releases/archives/facts_for_features_special_editions/cb11-ff22.html.

21 Alexis de Tocqueville, *Democracy in America*, vols. 1 and 2, trans. Henry Reeve (New York: Barnes and Noble Publishers, 2003 [1862]), p. 311.

A NOTE ON THE TYPE

THE NEW TRAIL OF TEARS has been set in Le Monde Livre. Designed in 1997 by Jean-François Porchez, Le Monde Livre adapts for book typography the award-winning 1994 type family Porchez created for France's Le Monde *newspaper, types now called Le Monde Journal. While the Journal types were specifically intended to be used at small sizes, the Livre family is suitable for larger, less dense settings planned for longer reading. The family was subsequently expanded with a more decorative variation (Le Monde Classic) and a sans-serif (Le Monde Sans). Graced with both style and readability, all of the Le Monde types display Porchez's considerable skill as a designer of typefaces and his deep knowledge of typographic history, particularly the rich heritage of French types from the sixteenth through nineteenth centuries.*

DESIGN & COMPOSITION BY CARL W. SCARBROUGH